expectations
investing

expectations investing

reading stock prices for better returns

ALFRED RAPPAPORT
MICHAEL J. MAUBOUSSIN

HARVARD BUSINESS SCHOOL PRESS
BOSTON, MASSACHUSETTS

Requests for permission to use or reproduce material from this book should be directed to permissions@hbsp.harvard.edu, or mailed to Permissions, Harvard Business School Publishing, 60 Harvard Way, Boston, Massachusetts 02163.

Library of Congress Cataloging-in-Publication Data
Rappaport, Alfred.
    Expectations investing : reading stock prices for better returns / Alfred Rappaport, Michael J. Mauboussin.
       p. cm.
    Includes bibliographical references and index.
    ISBN 1-57851-252-2 (alk. paper)
    1. Investment analysis.   2. Portfolio management.   3. Stocks—Prices.   I. Mauboussin, Michael J., 1964–   II. Title.
HG4529 .R37 2000
332.63'2042—dc21

2001024378

The paper used in this publication meets the requirements of the American National Standard for Permanence of Paper for Publications and Documents in Libraries and Archives Z39.48-1992.

To Sharon

To Michelle

contents

Greater Expectations: How Investing Differs
   from Art Collecting by Peter L. Bernstein   xi
Preface   xv
Acknowledgments   xix

1   **The Case for Expectations Investing**   1
    Active Management: Challenge and Opportunity   4
    The Expectations Investing Process   7
    The Twilight of Traditional Analysis   8
    Essential Ideas   14
    Appendix: Earnings Growth and Value Creation   15

Part I   **Gathering the Tools**   17
    2   **How the Market Values Stocks**   19
      The Right Expectations   19
      Shareholder-Value Road Map   21
      Free Cash Flow   22
      Cost of Capital   28
      Forecast Period   33
      From Corporate Value to Shareholder Value   33
      Summary Illustration   34
      Essential Ideas   35
      Appendix: Estimating Residual Value   36
      The Perpetuity Method   36
      The Perpetuity-with-Inflation Method   37

3   The Expectations Infrastructure   39
     The Expectations Infrastructure   40
     Not All Expectations Revisions Are Equal   46
     Essential Ideas   49

4   Analyzing Competitive Strategy   51
     The Dual Uses of Competitive Strategy Analysis   51
     Historical Analysis   52
     Competitive Strategy Frameworks   53
     Essential Ideas   65

Part II   Implementing the Process   67

5   How to Estimate Price-Implied Expectations   69
     Reading Expectations   71
     Gateway Case Study   73
     Why Revisit Expectations?   76
     Essential Ideas   76
     Appendix: Employee Stock Options and
          Expectations Investing   78
     Valuing ESOs   78

6   Identifying Expectations Opportunities   85
     Searching for Expectations Opportunities   86
     Pitfalls to Avoid   90
     Gateway Case Study   92
     Essential Ideas   104

7   Buy, Sell, or Hold?   105
     Expected-Value Analysis   105
     Gateway Case Study   108
     The Buy Decision   110
     The Sell Decision   112
     The Role of Taxes   114
     Essential Ideas   115

8   Beyond Discounted Cash Flow   117
     Real Options   118
     When to Use Real-Options Analysis in
          Expectations Investing   125

The Value of Real Options in Amazon.com   128
Reflexivity   132
Essential Ideas   134

9   **Across the Economic Landscape**   135
    Business Categories   136
    Business Categories and the Value Factors   140
    Essential Ideas   149

Part III   Reading Corporate Signals   151

10 **Mergers and Acquisitions**   153
    How Acquiring Companies Add Value   154
    Evaluating Synergies   155
    What to Do When a Deal Is Announced   157
    Essential Ideas   168

11 **Share Buybacks**   171
    The Golden Rule of Share Buybacks   173
    Four Popular Motivations for Share Buybacks   175
    Essential Ideas   183

12 **Incentive Compensation**   185
    CEO and Other Corporate-Level Executives   186
    Operating-Unit Executives   191
    Middle Managers and Frontline Employees   193
    Essential Ideas   195

    Notes   197
    Index   213
    About the Authors   223

greater expectations
how investing differs
from art collecting

Peter L. Bernstein

How does the capitalist system *really* work? In *Capital*, Karl Marx uses a remarkably simple equation to answer this question: M-C-M'. In words, the capitalist starts with *M*oney, converts it into *C*apital, and ends up with *M*ore Money than he had originally. Note that money appears at both the beginning and the end of this equation. Note, also, that Marx does not describe a system in which the capitalist starts with money and then ends up with capital worth more than the original investment. Marx knew how to avoid that trap. If capital can never produce a flow of cash to its owners, then it is worthless, intrinsically and as a practical matter.

A century and a quarter after the publication of *Capital*, Jack Welch, the legendary CEO of General Electric and capitalist supreme, displayed his own recognition of M' as the driving force at GE—although the intellectual roots of how he perceived the corporate goal might surprise him. In the company's 1995 annual report, Welch explained that GE was "a company whose only answer to the trendy question, 'What do you intend to spin off?' is '*cash—and lots of it.*'"

Al Rappaport and Michael Mauboussin also fully appreciate the overarching importance of cash. The seminal concept of M' forms the core of their extraordinary book. In crystal-clear language, they capture

xii   greater expectations

the full spirit of Marx's and Welch's emphasis on cash and employ it to develop a unique and powerful structure for investment strategies.

Had Marx limited his mathematical description of capitalism only to M-C, what purpose could such capital possibly serve? Without a monetary return, the owners of a firm could not pay for their groceries, opera tickets, Mercedes limousines, and Park Avenue apartments. Without money, they could pay for nothing. Even someone who would accept shares of a company as a stock dividend or in payment for a merger or acquisition would have to visualize a flow of cash somewhere, some time in the future. Any other expectation would be irrational; only people who collect objects like old stock certificates or works of art would expect anything else.

Indeed, without the prospect of cash flows, corporate assets would resemble bars of gold or zero-coupon bonds of infinite maturity, assets whose values are set only by the whims of the market (otherwise known as other investors), with no anchors, no tangibility, no *meaning*. I alluded above to art collectors to make this point: The process for pricing assets that will never produce a flow of cash to their owners parallels the process for valuing art or betting on horse races. Why is one painting worth millions of dollars and another worth a few hundred? No calculations can answer that question; the owner merely hopes that another art collector will step up to justify today's selling price at some point in the future.

Assets producing cash flows will ultimately return the owner's investment without depending on the whims of other investors. Even if those cash flows are some distance in the future, their prospects endow them with a present value. Financial markets are nothing more than arenas where investors who need cash today can obtain it by selling the present value of future cash flows to other investors willing to wait for the cash payoffs from their capital. The payment medium in this transaction is *money*. The crucial point: If you invest without expecting future cash flows, then you might as well collect art or play the slot machines.

The tension in this book demands our attention. It focuses on future cash flows, but we never know for certain what the future holds. We cannot even count on the cash flows from U.S. Treasury obligations—

perhaps less uncertain than other cash flows, but uncertain neverthe-less. *The fundamental law of investing is the uncertainty of the future.*

How, then, can a rational investor derive the value of a future stream of cash, even a contractual one such as promised in a debt instrument? Rappaport and Mauboussin walk their way around this question by telling their readers *not* to answer it. I kid you not. Instead, the authors advise readers to let other investors answer the question! And their answers come through, loud and clear, in the prices paid for financial assets in the capital markets. As Rappaport and Mauboussin remind us repeatedly, stock prices (and bond prices, too) are a gift from the mar-ket, a gift of information about how other investors with money on the line are estimating the value of future cash flows.

If the market's generosity in providing key information were the whole story, then the authors would have written a pamphlet instead of a plump volume. But the market price is only the beginning, not the end. Investors still have hard work to do. We may be able to glean what other investors expect, but we should not accept those expectations without qualification. We must test the beliefs of the market, and here Rappaport and Mauboussin are at their best. They set forth a systematic testing process to guide the investor toward a reasoned judgment about both the company involved and the market's expectations, ultimately to determine whether to buy, sell, or hold.

Long experience in the capital markets reveals few lessons valid for all times; but, in half a century as a professional investor, I have found one particularly robust: The secret of success in maximizing the treas-ures of instruction in this book is *silence*. This important piece of advice to investors applies especially to *Expectations Investing.*

You need no ears to carry out the method recommended by Rappa-port and Mauboussin. You can easily find everything you need, in print or on the Internet, specifically in market prices that reflect the views of investors willing to put their money where their mouths are, in publicly available corporate financial statements, and in the consensus forecasts published by reputable sources. Armed with this assemblage of data, you need not listen to the cacophony of recommendations flooding the investment community every minute of every day, no matter how excit-ing or lofty the sources of those recommendations. You can follow the *actions* of investors, not the *advice* of the gurus. The more you succeed in shutting your ears to all the other voices assailing investors, the more you will succeed in your investing. Let your eyes, not your ears, inform your brain.

Reading the tea leaves as described by Rappaport and Mauboussin is no simple task, although their recommended process is direct and uncluttered. No method of security selection will ever guarantee you success in a dynamic economy where the future always eludes you. The trick is to know where you are going, why you are going there, and why you must ignore any approach that lacks a logical path to the heart of value. The methodology of *Expectations Investing* meets all three requirements. As I suggested above, don't confuse stock picking with art collecting.

preface

Stock prices are the clearest and most reliable signal of the market's expectations about a company's future performance. The key to successful investing is to estimate the level of expected performance embedded in the current stock price and then to assess the likelihood of a revision in expectations. Investors who properly read market expectations and anticipate revisions increase their odds of achieving superior investment results. The expectations investing process allows you to identify the *right* expectations and effectively anticipate revisions in a company's prospects.

The expectations investing process represents a fundamental shift from the way professional money managers and individual investors select stocks today. This book presents both the compelling benefits for expectations investing as well as the tools that investors need to implement it for all publicly traded stocks—old- and new-economy stocks, value and growth stocks, as well as start-up stocks.

This book brings the power of expectations investing to portfolio managers, security analysts, investment advisers, individual investors, and business students. We believe that expectations investing will generate substantial interest in the corporate and the investment communities. After all, both investors and managers accept stock price as the "scorecard" for corporate performance. Companies seeking to outperform the Standard & Poor's 500 Index or an index of their peers can use expectations investing to establish the reasonableness of the goal.

Chapter 1 makes the case for expectations investing and explains why traditional analysis, with its focus on short-term earnings and price-earnings multiples, chases the wrong expectations. In "Gathering the Tools," part I of this book (chapters 2 through 4), we introduce all the tools you need to implement expectations investing. Chapter 2 shows that stock market expectations are based on a company's long-term cash flows; we demonstrate how to estimate shareholder value using this model. Chapter 3 introduces the expectations infrastructure, a powerful new tool to help investors understand the underlying sources of expectations revisions. Chapter 4 provides competitive strategy frameworks that you can apply to improve your odds of correctly anticipating expectations shifts.

Chapters 5 through 9 (part II, "Implementing the Process") address implementation issues. Chapters 5, 6, and 7—the core of the book—describe the three-step expectations investing process. Chapter 5 outlines the first step, showing you how to estimate the market expectations that justify a company's stock price. This step allows investors to harness the power of the discounted cash-flow model without the need for speculative, long-term forecasts. Chapter 6 integrates the tools from the first four chapters to identify potential expectations opportunities—that is, meaningful revisions from current expectations. Chapter 7, the final step of the process, establishes well-defined standards for buy, sell, and hold decisions. The three-step expectations investing process is all you need to conduct analysis for most companies. Certain start-up companies and established companies undergoing dramatic change and uncertainty require additional analysis because the cash flows from existing businesses do not even come close to justifying the stock price. Chapter 8 employs the real-options approach to estimating the potential value of uncertain future opportunities for these companies. Chapter 9 classifies companies into three business categories—physical, service, and knowledge. While each category has distinct characteristics, we show expectations investing is applicable to all companies across the economic landscape.

Finally, in chapters 10 through 12 (part III, "Reading Corporate Signals"), we examine three corporate transactions—mergers and acquisitions, share buybacks, and incentive compensation—that involve stock and often provide important signals to investors. Specifically, we show how decisions to finance acquisitions, to repurchase stock, and to use stock options for incentive compensation can reveal management's view of the company's prospects compared to the market's expectations.

Please visit us at www.expectationsinvesting.com.

acknowledgments

A number of people read segments of early versions of the manuscript and provided valuable suggestions. Our deepest appreciation goes to David Besanko, Jack Cieslielski, Martin L. Leibowitz, Timothy A. Luehrman, William Miller III, Thomas Nodine, and Richard Thaler. We extend our very special gratitude to Martha Amram, who generously contributed key insights and clarified our discussion of real options in chapter 8 while enriching our understanding of the subject.

We are indebted to current and former Credit Suisse First Boston employees for providing resources and encouragement throughout the project. In particular we thank Jane Adams, Terrence Cuskley, Brady Dougan, Jay Freedman, Bob Hiler, Al Jackson, Paul Johnson, Stephen Kawaja, Steve Kraus, Laura Martin, Patrick McCarthy, Michael Regan, Alexandar Schay, and Charlie Wolf.

Special thanks go to Melissa Little, who not only helped prepare the manuscript but also took care of all the other little things—with unrelenting cheerfulness and professionalism.

We received very helpful input from L.E.K. Consulting, including partners Marc Kozin, Leon Schor, and John Thomas, as well as Advisory Board members Harry M. Jansen Kraemer, Jr., James Lawrence, Wayne Lowell, Robert Roath, Neal Schmale, and Alan Shapiro. We both have greatly benefited from our association with L.E.K.—Rappaport as a research consultant to the firm and Mauboussin as a member of the Advisory Board.

As a member of the faculty for twenty-eight years at the J. L. Kellogg Graduate School of Management, Northwestern University, Rappaport would like to acknowledge the benefits of its extraordinarily stimulating teaching and research environment. Also, his association with The Alcar Group, Inc., which he co-founded with Carl M. Noble, Jr., in 1979, was instrumental in learning how to translate shareholder value from theory to organizational reality.

We owe many thanks to the Harvard Business School Press team, in particular to our editor Kirsten Sandberg, whose insightful guidance meaningfully strengthened the manuscript, and to Carol Franco, Director of HBS Press, who enthusiastically committed the Press to the success of the book. Our thanks also go to manuscript editor Jane Judge Bonassar, who with great professionalism and good cheer helped us navigate through the process of multiple revisions, and to Penny Stratton and Patty Boyd, whose editing suggestions helped sharpen the manuscript.

We have admired Peter Bernstein's scholarly and practical writings for many years, and are deeply honored that he consented to write the foreword to this book.

Finally, we enjoyed invaluable support from our families. Al thanks his wife, Sharon, and his sons, Nort and Mitch. Michael thanks his wife, Michelle; his parents; his mother-in-law, Andrea Maloney-Schara; and his wonderful children, Andrew, Alex, Madeline, and Isabelle.

expectations
investing

1

the case for expectations investing

Flip on CNBC or read any popular business magazine, and you'll get a familiar story. The growth money manager will explain that she looks for well-managed companies that have rapidly growing earnings but that trade at reasonable price-earnings multiples. The value manager will extol the virtues of buying quality companies at low price-earnings multiples. It happens every day.

But think for a moment about what these investors are really saying. When the growth manager buys a stock, she's betting that the stock market isn't fully capturing the company's growth prospects. The value manager bets that the market is underestimating the company's value. In both cases, they believe that the market's current expectations are incorrect and are likely to be revised upward.

Although investors invariably talk about expectations, they're usually talking about the *wrong* expectations. The errors fall into two camps. Either investors don't appreciate the *structure* of expectations, or they do a poor job of *benchmarking* expectations.

An example of a faulty structure is a near-messianic focus on short-term earnings. As it turns out, short-term earnings are not very helpful

1

for gauging expectations because they are a poor proxy for how the market values stocks. Yet even the investors who do embrace an appropriate economic model often miss the mark because they fail to benchmark their expectations against those of the market. Without knowing where expectations are today, it is hard to know where they are likely to go tomorrow.

The central theme of this book is that the ability to properly read market expectations and anticipate revisions of these expectations is the springboard for superior returns—long-term returns above an appropriate benchmark. Stock prices express the collective expectations of investors, and changes in these expectations determine your investment success.

Seen in this light, stock prices are gifts of information—expectations—waiting for you to unwrap and use. If you've got a fix on current expectations, then you can figure out where they are likely to go. Like the great hockey player Wayne Gretzky, you can learn to "skate to where the puck is going to be, not where it is."[1] That's expectations investing.

In a sharp break from standard practice, *expectations investing* is a stock-selection process that uses the market's own pricing model, the discounted cash-flow model, with an important twist: Rather than forecast cash flows, expectations investing *starts* by reading the expectations implied by a company's stock price.[2] It also reveals how revisions in expectations affect value. Simply stated, expectations investing uses the right tools to assess the right expectations to determine the right investment move.

Why now? We need to integrate price-implied expectations into our investment decisions because the stakes are now higher than ever. Consider the following:

- Over 50 million U.S. households—nearly one in two—own mutual funds. Many more individuals participate in the stock market directly through stock ownership and self-directed retirement accounts, or indirectly through pension programs. Around the globe, expectations investing can provide investors with a complete stock-selection framework or, at a minimum, a useful standard by which they can judge the decisions of their portfolio managers.

- Investors quickly withdraw money from poorly performing funds. Money managers who use outdated analytical tools risk performing poorly and losing funds. Expectations investing applies across the economic landscape (old and new economy) and across investment styles (growth and value).

- Lured by reduced trading costs, better access to information, the disappointing record of active managers, and the fun of managing money, many individual investors are shunning actively managed mutual funds and overseeing their own investments. In fact, individuals managed over 28 million online trading accounts in the United States in 2000, and online trades exceeded one-third of retail trading volume in equities. If you currently manage your investments or are considering the possibility, then expectations investing can improve your odds of achieving superior performance.

- More than ever before, major corporate decisions such as merger-and-acquisition (M&A) financing, share buybacks, and employee stock options rely on an intelligent assessment of a company's stock price. These decisions to issue or repurchase shares might signal the market to revise its expectations. Expectations investing provides a way to read management's decisions and anticipate revisions in market expectations.

Expectations investing is a practical application of sound theory that many companies have used over the past couple of decades. The process includes the principles of value creation and competitive strategy analysis. We tailor these tools specifically for investors, creating a new integrated power tool kit for investors.

Succeeding at active investing will only get harder. With an accelerating rate of innovation, greater global interdependence, and vast information flows, uncertainty has notably increased. We believe that expectations investing can translate this heightened uncertainty into opportunity. Further, the U.S. Securities and Exchange Commission Regulation FD ("fair disclosure"), implemented in late 2000, requires companies to disclose material information to all investors simultaneously so that no one gets an informational edge.

ACTIVE MANAGEMENT:
CHALLENGE AND OPPORTUNITY

Most active managers (both institutional and individual) generate returns on their investment portfolios lower than those of passive funds that mirror broader market indexes such as the Standard & Poor's 500 Composite (S&P 500). In fact, about three-quarters of active professional managers lag the passive benchmark in an average year, a remarkably constant statistic over time.[3]

Investment performance is a zero-sum game: For every investor who beats the market, another underperforms it. In such a world, we expect the skilled investors to gain and the unskilled to lose. Thus the underperformance of the talented investment pros is baffling. Peter Bernstein, one of the investment world's most astute observers, notes that since 1984, the top quintile of professional fund managers have beat the S&P 500 by a narrower margin than in the past.[4] Meanwhile, the bottom quintile performers have lagged by margins as great or greater than before.

Why do institutional investors underperform passive benchmarks? Does active management really pay? If so, then what approach offers the best chance of superior returns?

Before we address these questions, here's the bottom line: *The disappointing performance of professionally managed funds is not an indictment of active management; rather, it reflects the suboptimal strategies that active pros use. Expectations investing offers the best available process to achieve superior returns.*

Let's be clear. Active investing is not for the fainthearted. If you want to avoid underperforming the market, and if broad market returns will satisfy you, then you should choose low-cost index funds. Even the most astute and diligent investors struggle to beat the market consistently over time, and expectations investing offers no shortcut to riches. But its approach will help all active investors to meet their potential.

Now let's look at the four primary reasons that institutional investors underperform passive benchmarks—tools, costs, incentives, and style limitations—and see how expectations investing alleviates these constraints.

Tools

Standard practice: Most investors use accounting-based tools, like short-term earnings and price-earnings multiples. These inherently flawed measures are becoming even less useful as companies increasingly depend on intangible rather than tangible assets to create value. We expand on the shortcomings of earnings as poor proxies for market expectations in the last section of this chapter.

Expectations investing draws from modern finance theory to pinpoint the market's expectations. It then taps appropriate competitive strategy frameworks to help investors anticipate revisions in expectations.

Costs

Standard practice: John Bogle, founder of The Vanguard Group, correlates costs to mutual fund performance, averring that "the surest route to top-quartile performance is bottom-quartile expenses."[5] Annual operating and management investment expenses for equity funds average about 1.5 percent of asset value. In addition, mutual funds pay broker commissions of another 1 percent or so because of high portfolio turnover. With total costs that average about 2.5 percent per year, investors earn only 75 percent of an annual long-term return of 10 percent—excluding the impact of taxes. In contrast, index funds have lower operating expenses and relatively low transaction costs.[6]

Expectations investing establishes demanding standards for buying and selling stocks, resulting in lower stock portfolio turnover, reduced transaction costs, and lower taxes.

Incentives

Standard practice: Fund shareholders generally compare their returns quarterly to a benchmark, usually the S&P 500. Fund managers often fear that, if they fail to achieve acceptable short-term performance, then they will lose substantial assets, their jobs, and, ultimately, the opportunity to achieve superior long-term returns. Naturally, these managers obsess over short-term relative returns. If they shift from identifying mispriced stocks to minimizing the variance from the benchmark, then they blunt their odds of outperforming index funds.

Expectations investing improves the probability of beating the benchmark over longer periods, provided that the fund manager can buck the system and embrace more effective analytical tools.

Style Limitations

Standard practice: Most professional money managers classify their investing style as either "growth" or "value." Growth managers seek companies that rapidly increase sales and profits and generally trade at high price-earnings multiples. Value managers seek stocks that trade at substantial discounts to their expected value and often have low price-earnings multiples. Significantly, fund industry consultants discourage money managers from drifting from their stated style, thus limiting their universe of acceptable stocks.

Expectations investing doesn't distinguish between growth and value; managers simply pursue maximum long-term returns within a specified investment policy. As Warren Buffett convincingly argues, "Market commentators and investment managers who glibly refer to 'growth' and 'value' styles as contrasting approaches to investment are displaying their ignorance, not their sophistication. Growth is simply a component—usually a plus, sometime a minus—in the value equation."[7]

Further, not only does expectations investing help identify undervalued stocks to buy or hold, it also identifies overvalued *stocks to avoid or sell* in the investor's target universe.

Does expectations investing offer insightful, dedicated investors a reasonable probability of achieving superior returns? We think so.

In 1976, Jack Treynor distinguished "between ideas whose implications are obvious" and those "that require reflection, judgment, and special expertise for their evaluation." The latter ideas, he argued, are "the only meaningful basis for long-term investing."[8] When companies announce earnings surprises, mergers and acquisitions, a new drug, or a government antitrust action, the long-term valuation implications are rarely obvious. Investors quickly assess the effects, favorable or unfavorable, on current price, and they trade accordingly. Not surprisingly, trading volume typically increases after these announcements. Volatile stock prices and increased trading volume affirm that investors quickly respond to such information. But what distinguishes the winners from the losers is not how quickly they respond, but how well they *interpret* the information. Different investors interpret the same information differently, and some interpretations are much better than others.

In other words, stock prices quickly reflect revised but perhaps misguided expectations; therefore, to succeed, investors must first skillfully read expectations and then use the best available tools to decide whether and how today's expectations will change. Welcome to expectations investing.

THE EXPECTATIONS INVESTING PROCESS

In the following chapters, we'll walk you carefully through the three-step process of expectations investing.

Step 1: Estimate Price-Implied Expectations

We first "read" the expectations embedded in a stock with a long-term discounted cash-flow model. We thus reverse the common practice, which begins with earnings or cash-flow forecasts to estimate value. The benefits of this reverse engineering include the following:

- The long-term discounted cash-flow model is the right tool to read expectations because it mirrors the way the market prices stocks.

- Expectations investing solves a dilemma that investors face in a world of heightened uncertainty by allowing them to harness the power of the discounted cash-flow model without forecasting long-term cash flows.

Step 2: Identify Expectations Opportunities

Once we estimate current expectations, we then apply the appropriate strategic and financial tools within a tightly integrated competitive-strategy analysis and finance framework to determine where and when revisions in expectations are likely to occur. Here are the advantages of this approach:

- Expectations investing methodology reveals whether the stock price is most sensitive to expectations revisions in the company's sales, operating costs, or investment needs so that investors can focus on the potential revisions that affect price most.

- Expectations investing applies the best available competitive-strategy frameworks in the investor's search for potential expectations revisions.

- Expectations investing provides the tools to evaluate *all* public companies—old and new economy, value and growth, developed and emerging market, start-up and established. Expectations investing applies universally.

Step 3: Buy, Sell, or Hold?

Finally, the process defines clear standards for buy and sell decisions. Central features include the following:

- Prospective buys or sells must offer a clear-cut "margin of safety." A buy candidate, for example, must trade at a sufficient discount to its expected value.

- Key insights from behavioral finance help investors avoid decision-making pitfalls.

- The use of demanding buy and sell hurdles reduces transaction costs and income taxes.

THE TWILIGHT OF TRADITIONAL ANALYSIS

In 1938, John Burr Williams published *The Theory of Investment Value*, a seminal articulation of the usefulness of the discounted cash-flow model to establish value. Williams convincingly addressed investor concerns that the long-term discounted flow model is too intricate, uncertain, and impractical.[9] Notwithstanding the extraordinary advances in financial theory since then, many investors still eschew the model and the full cadre of available financial and strategic tools to implement it.

The full demonstration of expectations investing in the following chapters will reveal its analytical superiority to widely used investment tools. But three pervasive misconceptions in the investment community deserve special mention:

1. The market is short-term.

2. Earnings per share (EPS) dictate value.

3. Price-earnings multiples determine value.

These fallacies lead investors to chase the wrong expectations, frequently resulting in poor performance. Let's examine each.

BELIEF: The Market Is Short-Term
REALITY: The Market Takes the Long View

Most investors (and corporate managers) believe that short-term reported earnings rather than long-term cash flows fuel stock prices. Why? There are three plausible explanations.

The first is a misinterpretation of the stock market's response to earnings announcements. When quarterly earnings announcements provide investors with *new* information about a company's long-term cash-flow prospects, the stock price changes. But the market does not react mechanically to reported earnings. Rather, it uses unexpected earnings results as a signal to revise expectations for a company's future cash flows when appropriate. If the market interprets a disappointing earnings announcement as a sign of a longer-term downturn, then it drives the stock price down.[10]

Second, the stocks of businesses with excellent long-term prospects do not always deliver superior shareholder returns. If a company's stock price fully anticipates its performance, then shareholders should expect to earn a normal, market-required rate of return. The only investors who earn superior returns are those who correctly *anticipate changes* in a company's competitive position (and the resulting cash flows) that the current stock price does not reflect.

Finally, commentators frequently point to short (and shortening) investor holding periods to support their belief that the market is short-term. John Bogle notes that the average holding period for funds has plummeted from about seven years in the mid-1960s to just over a year by 2000.[11] How can investors who hold stock for months, or days, care about a company's long-term outlook?

This conundrum has a simple solution: *Investor holding periods differ from the market's investment time horizon.* To understand the horizon, you must look at stock prices, not investor holding periods. Studies confirm that you must extend expected cash flows over many years to justify stock prices. Investors make short-term bets on long-term outcomes.

How do we know that the market takes the long view? The most direct evidence comes from stock prices themselves: We can estimate the expected level and duration of cash flows that today's price implies. As it turns out, most companies need over ten years of value-creating cash flows to justify their stock price.

Indirect evidence comes from the percentage of today's stock price that we can attribute to dividends expected over the next five years. Only about 10 to 15 percent of the price of stocks in the Dow Jones Industrial Average results from expected dividends for the next five years.[12]

BELIEF: Earnings per Share Dictate Value
REALITY: Earnings Tell Us Little About Value

The investment community undeniably fixates on EPS. The *Wall Street Journal* and other financial publications amply cover quarterly earnings, EPS growth, and price-earnings multiples. This broad dissemination and frequent market reactions to earnings announcements might lead some to believe that reported earnings strongly influence, if not totally determine, stock prices.

The profound differences between earnings and long-term cash flows, however, not only underscore why earnings are such a poor proxy for expectations, but also show why upward earnings revisions do not necessarily increase stock price. The shortcomings of earnings include the following:

• Earnings exclude a charge for the cost of capital.

• Earnings exclude the incremental investments in working capital and fixed capital needed to support a company's growth.

• Companies can compute earnings using alternative, equally acceptable accounting methods.

Discounted cash-flow models, and stock prices, account for the time value of money: A dollar today is worth more than a dollar a year from now because we can invest today's dollar to earn a return over the next year. So when a company invests, it must compare its return to those of alternative, equally risky investment opportunities. This opportunity cost, or cost of capital, is the discount rate for a discounted cash-flow model. Earnings calculations, in contrast, ignore this opportunity cost.

In a discounted cash-flow model, value increases only when the company earns a rate of return on new investments that exceeds the cost of capital. *However, a company can grow earnings without investing at or above the cost of capital.* (See the appendix at the end of this chapter for a detailed example.) Consequently, higher earnings do not always translate into higher value.

Consider the second difference—the required investments in working capital and fixed capital. Earnings do not recognize the cash outflows for investments in future growth, such as increases in accounts receivable, inventory, and fixed assets. Discounted cash-flow models, in contrast, consider all cash inflows and outflows. The Home Depot's fiscal 1999 net income was $2,320 million, whereas its cash flow was only $35 million (table 1-1). What does the first figure tell you about the second one, in either the near or the long term? Very little.

An analysis of cash flow as a percentage of net income for the thirty Dow Jones Industrial Average companies shows a similar result: Cash flow was about 80 percent of earnings for the group, and earnings exceeded cash flow for twenty-three of the thirty companies.[13]

Finally, companies can use a wide range of permissible methods to determine earnings. How accountants record a business event does not alter the event or its impact on shareholder value.

Enlightened accountants readily acknowledge that neither they nor their conventions have a comparative advantage in valuing a business. The role of corporate financial reporting is to provide useful information *for* estimating value.

Two fundamental steps—revenue recognition and matching expenses with revenue—determine earnings. A company recognizes revenue when it delivers products or services and can reasonably establish the amount that it will collect from customers. It then expenses the costs needed to generate that revenue during the period in which it recognizes the revenue. In other words, it matches expenses with revenues. This matching principle is easy to grasp in concept but hopelessly arbitrary in implementation.

Accounting standards give companies latitude in revenue recognition, depreciation methods, and inventory accounting, to name a few. Multibillion-dollar restructuring charges create "cookie jar" reserves that companies can use to fuel future, illusory earnings. Finally, earnings exclude the cost of employee stock options. We present the steps to value them in chapter 5.

Notwithstanding the shortcomings of earnings, Wall Street loves playing the earnings expectations game. It's just the *wrong* expectations game to play.

Here are the basic rules of the earnings game and why it is a lose-lose proposition for investors and managers.

TABLE 1-1   Reconciliation of Earnings and Cash Flow for The Home Depot (1999, in millions)

	Earnings	Adjustment	Cash Flow
Sales	$ 38,434		
+ Decrease in receivables		85	$ 38,519
Cost of merchandise sold	(27,023)		
+ Increase in inventories		1,142	(28,165)
Selling, general, and administrative expenses	(7,616)		
− Increase in payables		795	(6,821)
+ Depreciation expense		463	463
− Capital expenditures		2,581	(2,581)
Interest, net	9		9
Income taxes	(1,484)		
−Increase in income taxes payable		95	(1,389)
Net income	**$ 2,320**		
Cash flow			**$ 35**

Source: The Home Depot 1999 Annual Report.

Analysts have to guess how much a company will earn each quarter. But a company is allowed to provide the analysts with clues, or so-called guidance, about what it thinks earnings will be. This guidance number usually shows up as the consensus estimate among analysts. If the company's actual earnings meet or just beat the consensus, both the company and the analysts win: The stock goes up, and everyone looks smart. The game might not sound so hard, but it requires a lot of cooperation. Companies are under enormous pressure to achieve the consensus earnings estimates, while analysts rely on those same companies to help them form their earnings expectations in the first place.[14]

Companies have two levers in this game. They can manage expectations, manage earnings, or do both. To manage expectations, they guide analysts to an earnings number that the company can beat. And to beat expectations easily, companies often downplay their near-term prospects.

If a company can't meet or beat expectations, then it can either manage expectations downward or manage earnings. Flexible accounting conventions often allow managers to avoid unfavorable earnings surprises even amid an unexpected slowdown in business. Not surprisingly, about 20 percent of the S&P 500 companies beat the consensus earnings estimate by just a penny in a typical quarter and most earnings surprises are positive. Investors must separate companies that genuinely achieve better-than-expected operating performance from those that skillfully manage expectations and earnings.[15]

The earnings expectations game has two unintended consequences. First, it induces security analysts to fixate on quarterly earnings estimates at the expense of independent analysis. This fixation reduces the value of Wall Street research. Second, it causes managers to mislead themselves in a misguided attempt to please investors. The smooth progression of *reported* earnings can mask fundamental business problems that require urgent managerial attention. Left unattended, these problems inevitably lead to downward revisions of market expectations.

BELIEF: Price-Earnings Multiples Determine Value
REALITY: Price-Earnings Multiples Are a Function of Value

The investment community's favorite valuation metric is the price-earnings (P/E) multiple. A measure of what investors will pay for a stock, the multiple equals the stock price (P) divided by a company's earnings (E).[16] Investors incorporate it in a deceptively simple valuation formula:

Shareholder value per share = (Earnings per share) × (P/E)

Since an estimate of earnings per share (EPS) is available, investors must decide only on the appropriate multiple to determine a stock's value, then compare the result to the stock's current price and determine whether it is undervalued, overvalued, or fairly valued. The calculation is easy, but the results will surely disappoint.

Look at the formula closely. Since we know last year's EPS or next year's consensus EPS estimate, we need only to estimate the appropriate P/E. But since we have the denominator (earnings, or E), the only unknown is the appropriate share price, or P. We are therefore left with a useless tautology: *To estimate value, we require an estimate of value.*

This flawed logic underscores the fundamental point: *The price-earnings multiple does not determine value; rather, it derives from value.* Price-earnings analysis is not an analytic shortcut. It is an economic cul-de-sac.

ESSENTIAL IDEAS

- Investors who can read the market's expectations and anticipate changes in those expectations will more likely generate superior investment returns.

- The expectations investing approach harnesses the powerful discounted cash-flow model but starts with price and then solves for expectations.

- Investors who play the earnings expectations game are in a losing game because short-term earnings do not reflect how the market prices stocks.

Appendix: Earnings Growth and Value Creation

Why aren't earnings growth and shareholder value growth synonymous? Consider Earnings Growth, Incorporated (EGI). To simplify calculations, assume that EGI has no debt and requires no incremental investment. These simplifying assumptions do not affect the conclusions of the analysis. EGI's most recent year's income statement is as follows:

	($ in millions)
Sales	$100
Operating expenses	85
Operating profit (15%)	15
Taxes (40%)	6
Earnings	$ 9

Suppose the company maintains its present sales level and margins for the foreseeable future. With a 12 percent cost of equity capital, EGI's shareholder value is $9 million divided by 12 percent, or $75 million.

Now let's say that EGI has the opportunity to invest $7.5 million of its internally generated cash today, which will allow it to expand sales by 10 percent while maintaining pretax margins at 15 percent. Here is EGI's projected income statement for next year and subsequent years:

	($ in millions)
Sales	$110.0
Operating expenses	93.5
Operating profit (15%)	16.5
Taxes (40%)	6.6
Earnings	$ 9.9

EGI's shareholder value is now $82.5 million ($9.9 million divided by 12 percent) minus the $7.5 million investment, or $75 million ($82.5 − $7.5 = $75). Note that despite 10 percent earnings growth, shareholder value remains the same because the $7.5 million investment increases annual after-tax cash flow by $900,000 which, when discounted at 12 percent, is worth exactly $7.5 million. So when the present value of incremental cash inflow is identical to the present value of the cash outflow (investment), shareholder value doesn't change.

When new investments yield a return below the cost of capital, shareholder value decreases even as earnings increase. For example, assume that EGI's sales growth next year will be 20 percent with a $15 million investment. However, the pretax margin on incremental sales will be 10 percent, rather than the 15 percent rate projected earlier. Here is the revised income statement for next year and subsequent years:

	($ in millions)
Sales	$120
Operating expenses	103
Operating profit	17
Taxes (40%)	6.8
Earnings	$ 10.2

While earnings grow from $9 million to $10.2 million, or 13.33 percent, shareholder value goes to $70 million—$10.2 million divided by 12 percent, minus $15 million—a $5 million decrease.

Stock prices relate tenuously to earnings growth. Instead, *changes in expectations* about future cash flows drive changes in shareholder value and stock price. So reported earnings growth, even when accompanied by increases in shareholder value, can trigger reduced investor expectations and a fall in the stock price.

Part I

gathering

the tools

2

how the market
values stocks

With traditional discounted cash-flow analysis, you forecast cash flows to estimate a stock's value. Expectations investing reverses the process. It starts with a rich, underutilized source of information—the stock price—and determines the cash-flow expectations that justify that price. Those expectations, in turn, serve as the benchmark for buy, sell, or hold decisions.

Before we hike too far down the expectations investing path, we need to be certain that we are tracking the right expectations. We must therefore answer an essential question: Do prices in financial markets truly reflect expected future cash flows?

THE RIGHT EXPECTATIONS

We return to first principles to see why the stock market bases its expectations on long-term cash flows. A dollar today is worth more than a dollar in the future, because you can invest today's dollar and earn a positive rate of return, a process called *compounding*. The reverse of compounding is *discounting*, which converts a future cash flow into its equivalent present value. An asset's *present value* is the sum of its expected cash flows discounted by an expected rate of return—i.e., what investors expect to earn on assets with similar risk. The present value is the maximum price an investor should pay for an asset.[1]

The discounted cash-flow model sets prices in all well-functioning capital markets, including bonds and real estate. For example, bond issuers contractually establish a coupon rate, principal repayment, and maturity. Bond prices are, in fact, the present value of the contractual cash flows discounted at the current expected rate of return. When the inflationary outlook or a company's credit quality prompts a higher or lower expected rate, its bonds change price accordingly. The market sets prices so that expected returns match the perceived risk.

The discounted cash-flow model also dominates pricing in the commercial real estate market. When the Empire State Building went up for sale in the early 1990s, real estate experts pegged its market value at around $450 million—and yet the purchase price was a scant $40 million because of the building's long-term, below-market-rate master lease. Neither its marquee name nor its prime location set the Empire State Building's price. Its discounted cash-flow value did.[2]

Given that the magnitude, timing, and riskiness of cash flows determine the value of bonds and real estate, we can expect these variables to dictate stock prices as well, even though the inputs for stocks are much less certain. Whereas bonds contractually specify cash flows and a date when principal is repaid, stocks have uncertain cash flows, an indefinite life, and no provision for repayment. Because of the greater uncertainty, stocks are more difficult to value than bonds.

Does that mean that we shouldn't value stocks with discounted cash flow? Certainly not. After all, the returns that investors receive when they purchase any financial asset depend on the cash flows that they pocket while owning the asset plus their proceeds when selling it. John Bogle argues for discounted cash-flow valuation: "Sooner or later the rewards must be based on future cash flows. The purpose of any stock market, after all, is simply to provide liquidity for stocks in return for the promise of future cash flows, enabling investors to realize the present value of a future stream of income at any time."[3]

Extensive empirical research demonstrates that the market determines the prices of stocks just as it does any other financial asset. Specifically, the studies show two relationships. First, market prices respond to changes in a company's *cash-flow* prospects. Second, market prices reflect *long-term* cash-flow prospects. As noted in chapter 1, companies often need ten years of value-creating cash flows to justify their stock price. For companies with formidable competitive advantages, this period can last as long as thirty years.

Yet most money managers, security analysts, and individual investors avoid the difficulty of forecasting long-term cash flows altogether. Instead, they focus on near-term earnings, price-earnings multiples, and similar measures. Such measures can help identify undervalued stocks only when we can rely on them as proxies for a company's long-term cash-flow prospects. But static measures of near-term performance do not capture future performance, and ultimately they let investors down—especially in a global economy marked by spirited competition and disruptive technologies. Without assessing a company's future cash-flow prospects, investors cannot conclude that a stock is undervalued or overvalued.

SHAREHOLDER-VALUE ROAD MAP

Exactly what do we mean by "cash flow," and how does it determine shareholder value? Figure 2-1 depicts the straightforward process for estimating shareholder value.

Let's take a quick road trip. The shareholder-value road map shows the following relationships:

- Sales growth and operating profit margin determine operating profit.

- Operating profit minus cash taxes yields net operating profit after taxes (NOPAT).

- NOPAT minus investments in working and fixed capital equals free cash flow. Think of free cash flow as the pool of cash available to pay the claims of debt-holders and shareholders.

- Free cash flows discounted at the cost of capital determine corporate value.

- Corporate value plus nonoperating assets minus the market value of debt equals shareholder value.

The preceding relationships describe the standard discounted cash-flow process, which estimates cash flows to determine shareholder value. In contrast, expectations investing reverses the process by starting with price (which may differ from value) and determines the implied cash-flow expectations that justify that price.

FREE CASH FLOW

Conveniently, we can use familiar financial statement variables to estimate the market's expectations for future free cash flows. Take another look at figure 2-1. Three *operating value drivers*—sales growth, operating profit margin, and investment—and one *value determinant,* cash tax rate, determine free cash flow. Because management decisions significantly influence sales growth, operating profit margin, and incremental investment rate, we consider them operating value drivers and distin-

FIGURE 2-1   The Shareholder-Value Road Map

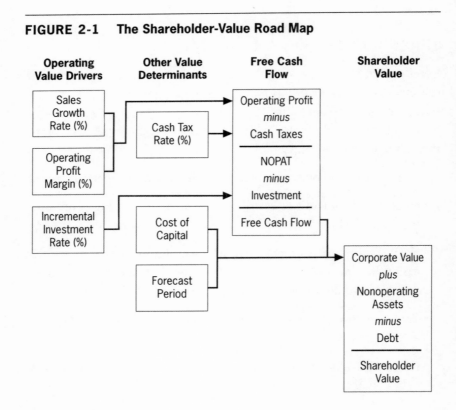

guish them from other value determinants, which external forces (the government, financial markets) dictate.

Here's how to calculate free cash flow for the first year of a forecast period. Assume that last year's sales were $100 million and that expectations for next year are as follows:

Sales growth rate	12%
Operating profit margin	10%
Cash tax rate	35%
Incremental fixed-capital investment	$1.20 million
Incremental working-capital investment	$0.60 million

We compute free cash flow as follows:

Sales	$112.00 million
Operating profit = Sales × Operating profit margin	
= 112.00 × 10%	11.20
Less: Cash taxes = Operating profit × Cash tax rate	
= 11.20 × 35%	(3.92)
NOPAT	7.28
Incremental fixed-capital investment	1.20
Incremental working-capital investment	0.60
Less: Total investment	(1.80)
Free cash flow	$ 5.48 million

The sales number is the same as the top line of the income statement. The sales growth rate is simply the year-to-year percentage change. Operating profit margin is the ratio of pre-interest, pretax operating profit to sales. Because we want to calculate cash flow, we exclude noncash expenses such as amortization of intangibles. Depreciation expense is part of the operating profit margin calculation, even though it is a noncash item. But we don't forget about it—we later deduct it from capital expenditures so that free cash flow is truly a "cash" figure.

On to taxes. The tax expense in the income statement, *book taxes*, is generally greater than the actual payments, or *cash taxes*, during a given period. Why? Because companies can recognize some revenue and expense items at different times for book versus tax purposes.

For example, a company may use straight-line depreciation for book purposes and an accelerated depreciation method for tax purposes.

Since accelerated depreciation is greater than straight-line depreciation, it increases a company's expenses and reduces its cash tax bill. As a result, cash tax rates are typically lower than book tax rates.[4] Table 2-1 shows average cash tax rates for various industries for the 1997–1999 period.

The cash tax rate represents taxes payable on operating profit, not on pretax income. Therefore, to calculate the taxes that a company would pay if it were entirely equity financed, we must remove the tax effects of interest expense and nonoperating income (or expenses). The tax benefit of interest expense deductions (interest expense multiplied by the tax rate) increases the cash tax bill, while the taxes on nonoperating income reduce the taxes on operating profit.

TABLE 2-1   Cash Tax Rate by Industry (Average for 1997–1999)

	Cash Tax Rate (%)
Basic materials	29.2
Capital goods	29.8
Consumer cyclicals	
Autos and auto parts	32.1
Retail	36.4
Consumer staples	
Beverages	30.0
Broadcasting	29.6
Food	35.3
Energy	29.4
Financials	27.0
Health care	
Biotechnology	29.9
Hospitals and nursing management	34.3
Medical specialties	39.8
Pharmaceuticals	28.5
Technology and telecommunications	
Computer processing hardware	33.9
Major telecommunications	30.7
Semiconductors	33.1
Software	32.5
Transportation	24.0
Utilities	31.0

Source: CSFB*Edge* database.

We now arrive at NOPAT (net operating profit after taxes). To complete the journey to free cash flow, we must subtract the incremental investments in fixed capital and working capital. Incremental investment captures *all* the company's investments (excluding expensed items)—not only routine capital expenditures and working-capital changes but also acquisitions. We must consider investments in all forms.

Let's begin with fixed capital investment. For insights into market expectations, we should use a publicly available service that provides long-term forecasts, such as Value Line Investment Survey and analyst projections, to estimate a company's *incremental fixed-capital investment rate,* that is, the fixed-capital investment required per dollar of sales increase. More specifically, we calculate the rate by dividing capital expenditures, minus depreciation expense, by the change in sales forecasted for the same period.[5] If this rate is, say, 10 percent, then a sales increase from $100 million to $112 million in the first year will produce an incremental fixed-capital investment of $1.20 million ($12 million × 10 percent = $1.20 million).

How useful are historical investment rates for assessing the reasonableness of expectations? The answer depends on the relative stability of a company's product mix, on technological changes, and on the company's ability to offset increased fixed-capital costs through higher selling prices or using fixed assets more efficiently. The historical investment rate, adjusted for relevant information, is a useful benchmark to assess the reasonableness of the forecasted rate.

Changes in operating working-capital relative to changes in sales define a company's *incremental working-capital investment rate.* The rate is the change, or incremental investment, in working capital expressed as a percentage of incremental sales. Operating working capital equals current assets (accounts receivable and inventory) minus non-interest-bearing current liabilities (accounts payable and accrued liabilities). As a business grows, operating working capital generally grows proportionally.

Changes in working capital underscore the difference between earnings and cash flow. For example, an increase in accounts receivable from the beginning to the end of a year indicates that a company received less cash during the year than the recorded sales suggest. For accounting purposes, companies recognize sales when they deliver goods or services, but for valuation purposes, what matters is when the companies receive cash.

Inventories also generally rise as sales increase. Rising inventory requires cash payments for materials, labor, and overhead. Since cost of goods sold excludes the cash outlays for additional inventory, we must include it as a working-capital investment.

The final components of working capital, accounts payable and accrued liabilities, counterbalance receivables and inventory. Payables and accrued liabilities represent unpaid bills for expenses already deducted on the income statement. Since companies disburse cash after they recognize some of their expenses, increases in payables reduce the current year's cash outlays and working-capital investment.

If the consensus rate is 5 percent, then the $12 million first-year increase in sales yields a $600,000 investment in working capital ($12 million × 5 percent = $600,000). Table 2-2 shows the average incremental fixed- and working-capital investment rates for various industries. Naturally, the rates for individual companies can differ significantly from the industry average.

The free cash flows over the forecast period represent only a fraction of a company's value. After all, a company has value at the end of the forecast period—its cash flows don't just mysteriously disappear at that time. *Residual value,* the value of post-forecast free cash flows, often constitutes most of a company's total value.

What is the best way to estimate residual value? We recommend either the *perpetuity method* or the *perpetuity-with-inflation method,* although perpetuity with inflation works better for most companies. Both approaches assume that a company generating returns greater than its cost of capital will attract competition, ultimately driving returns down to the cost of capital by the end of the forecast period. Further, both assume that a company can sustain the NOPAT it earns at the end of the forecast period and that future investments do not create value. The two methods do not suggest that a company will not grow. They do suggest that additional growth will not add shareholder value.

The perpetuity-with-inflation method assumes that free cash flow will grow at the inflation rate in the post-forecast period, which suggests that NOPAT remains level in *real* terms. In contrast, the perpetuity method implies that NOPAT remains constant in *nominal* terms. (The

appendix at the end of this chapter details the rationale and the calculation for the two methods.) No single residual value formula is appropriate in all circumstances; your assumptions about the business's competitive position at the end of the forecast period will determine which
method you choose.[6]

We now know how to take familiar financial statement metrics and
translate them into free cash flow. To convert free cash flows to corpo-

**TABLE 2-2   Incremental Fixed- and Working-Capital Investment
by Industry (Average for 1997–1999)**

	Incremental Fixed-Capital Rate (%)	Incremental Working-Capital Rate (%)	Total Investment Rate (%)
Capital goods	48	28	76
Consumer cyclicals			
Autos and auto parts	44	2	46
Retail	25	2	27
Consumer staples			
Beverages	43	4	47
Broadcasting	72	20	91
Food	24	2	27
Energy	263	3	266
Financials	13	N/A	13
Health care			
Biotechnology	42	−11	31
Hospitals and			
nursing management	47	59	106
Medical specialties	34	39	73
Pharmaceuticals	30	22	51
Technology and			
telecommunications			
Computer processing			
hardware	7	−6	0
Major telecommunications	168	2	170
Semiconductors	20	−9	11
Software	9	7	16
Transportation	146	−2	144
Utilities	96	3	98

Source: CSFB*Edge* database.

rate value, we need to estimate an appropriate discount rate—the cost of capital.

COST OF CAPITAL

The weighted average cost of capital, which includes both debt and equity, is the appropriate rate for discounting free cash flows. For example, suppose you estimate that a company's after-tax cost of debt is 4.3 percent and that its cost of equity is 11 percent. It plans to raise capital in the following proportion—15 percent debt and 85 percent equity. We calculate the cost of capital as follows:

	Weight (%)	Cost (%)	Weighted cost (%)
Debt (after-tax)	15	4.3	0.65
Equity	85	11.0	9.35
Cost of capital			10.00

The cost of capital incorporates the expected returns of both debt-holders and shareholders since both groups have claims on free cash flow. (Remember that free cash flow is *pre-interest*.) The weighted average cost of capital considers each group's claims in proportion to the targeted contribution to the financing of the company.

Should you use book (balance-sheet) value or market value to calculate weights for target capital structure? The answer is clearly market value, because debt-holders and shareholders expect to earn competitive rates of return on the market value of their stakes.[7] Book values reflect historical costs that generally do not correspond to market values and therefore are not relevant to today's investment decisions.

Table 2-3 shows the average mix of debt and equity for various industries. How do you estimate the costs of debt and equity? Since debt is a contractual obligation to pay a specific rate, measuring its cost is straightforward. It is the rate that a company would have to pay today on its long-term debt. Since interest expense on debt is tax deductible, the formula for finding the after-tax cost of debt-financed instruments to a company is this:

Yield-to-maturity on long-term debt × (1 − Tax rate)

Estimating the cost of equity is more difficult because companies do not explicitly agree to pay their common shareholders any particular rate of return. Nonetheless, investors require an *implicit* rate of return, or hurdle rate, to purchase or to hold a company's shares.

Rational, risk-averse investors expect to earn a rate of return proportionate with the risk they assume. Risk is, after all, the price that investors pay for opportunity. What rate of return is necessary to induce investors to buy a company's shares? One logical starting place is the

TABLE 2-3   Market Values of Debt and Equity as a Percentage of Total Capitalization (Average for 1997–1999)

	Debt (%)	Equity (%)
Basic materials	33	67
Capital goods	11	89
Consumer cyclicals		
Autos and auto parts	31	69
Retail	29	71
Consumer staples		
Beverages	25	75
Broadcasting	22	78
Food	28	72
Energy	28	72
Financials	4	96
Health care		
Biotechnology	5	95
Hospitals and nursing management	25	75
Medical specialties	18	82
Pharmaceuticals	8	92
Technology and telecommunications		
Computer processing hardware	8	92
Major telecommunications	25	75
Semiconductors	5	95
Software	3	97
Transportation	29	71
Utilities	46	54
Average of all industries	20	80

Source: CSFB*Edge* database.

sum of the risk-free rate—the yield of an appropriate government security is a good proxy—and an additional return for investing in more
risky stocks, or an *equity risk premium*.[8]

EQUATION 2-1
Cost of equity = Risk-free rate + Equity risk premium

Even government securities are not entirely risk-free. While essentially free of default risk, they are subject to increases in interest rates
and the resulting losses in value. In the absence of a truly riskless security, we can use the rate of return on long-term (ten-year) treasury
bonds, or comparable sovereign debt, to estimate the risk-free rate.

The equity risk premium is the second component of the cost of
equity. The equity risk premium for an individual stock is the product
of the market risk premium for equity and an individual stock's systematic risk as measured by its beta coefficient:[9]

EQUATION 2-2
Equity risk premium = Beta × Market risk premium

The *market risk premium* is the additional return that investors
expect for holding a well-diversified portfolio of stocks rather than risk-
free government bonds. To estimate the market risk premium, subtract
the risk-free rate from the expected rate of return on a representative
market index such as the Standard & Poor's 500:

EQUATION 2-3
Equity risk premium = Beta × (Expected market rate of return – Risk-free
rate)

Investors should base the market risk premium on *expected* rates of
return, not on historical rates, because the increased volatility of interest rates since the early 1980s has raised the relative risk of bonds and
lowered the market risk premium. Investors who use historical rates in
the 7 to 9 percent range ignore that market risk premiums vary over
time. Forward-looking approaches, as well as more recent historical
data, suggest an equity risk premium in the 3 to 5 percent range.[10]

The final variable, the *beta coefficient*, measures how sensitive a stock's return is to overall market movements. The beta on a market portfolio is 1.0. Stocks with betas greater than 1.0 are more volatile than the market, and thus have equity risk premiums greater than the market risk premium. For example, if a stock moves up or down 1.2 percent when the market moves up or down 1 percent, then it has a beta of 1.20. Likewise, stocks with positive betas of less than 1.0 move in the same direction as the market, but not as far. You can obtain betas from a number of sources, including Bloomberg, Barra, Merrill Lynch, Standard & Poor's, and Value Line. Table 2-4 shows average historical betas for various industries.

Equation 2-4 puts all the pieces together and provides the formula to calculate the cost of equity.

TABLE 2-4   Historical Industry Betas (as of October 2000)

	Average Beta
Basic materials	1.06
Capital goods	0.80
Consumer cyclicals	
Autos and auto parts	0.98
Retail	0.95
Consumer staples	
Beverages	0.61
Broadcasting	0.90
Food	0.68
Energy	0.90
Financials	1.17
Health care	
Biotechnology	0.92
Hospitals and nursing management	1.08
Medical specialties	0.78
Technology and telecommunications	
Computer processing hardware	1.22
Semiconductors	1.74
Software	1.39
Major telecommunications	1.20
Transportation	0.71

Source: Barra, Inc.

EQUATION 2-4

Cost of equity = Risk-free rate + Beta × (Expected market rate of return – Risk-free rate)

For example, if we assume a 6 percent risk-free rate, a beta of 1.25, and a 10 percent expected return on market, the cost of equity would be as follows:

Cost of equity = 6.0 + 1.25(10.0 – 6.0) = 11%

FINANCIAL INSTITUTIONS

In this chapter, we recommend that you use the enterprise discounted cash-flow method to read market expectations. This approach—which uses estimates of free cash flow to determine corporate value, adds cash and other nonoperating assets, and subtracts debt to calculate shareholder value—is appropriate for industrial companies.

In contrast, the best way for you to read expectations for financial service companies is with the equity discounted cash-flow method. Financial service companies, such as banks, insurance companies, and brokers, represent about 15 percent of the Standard & Poor's 500 Index. The equity approach discounts future free cash flows for shareholders at the cost of equity capital. Since financial service companies use the liability side of the balance sheet to create value, the equity approach, though mathematically equivalent to the enterprise method, is more straightforward.

Further, even within financial services, different business models require different approaches. For example, the model you need to read the expectations for a bank is different from what you need for an insurance company.

Despite these distinctions, however, the expectations investing techniques we develop throughout this book apply to all companies. You may need, however, to adapt the appropriate model slightly to best understand the expectations built into the stocks of financial service companies.

See Tom Copeland, Tim Koller, and Jack Murrin, *Valuation: Measuring and Managing the Value of Companies,* 3d ed. (New York: Wiley, 2000), 427–469; see also Aswath Damodoran, *Investment Valuation* (New York: Wiley, 1996), 219–234.

FORECAST PERIOD

To understand the importance of the forecast period, turn again to figure 2-1. Free cash flow discounted at the cost of capital determines today's value of future free cash flows. We now turn to the forecast period. How many years of free cash flow does the market impound in a stock price?

We disagree with valuation texts that advocate arbitrary five- or ten-year periods. The forecast period is the time that the *market* expects a company to generate returns on incremental investment that exceed its cost of capital. According to market-validated economic theory, companies that generate excess returns attract competition that eventually drives industry returns toward the cost of capital.

Analysts typically choose a forecast period that is too short when they perform discounted cash-flow valuations. If you believe that a forecast beyond two or three years smacks of sheer speculation, then you're missing the point. Market prices do reflect long-term cash-flow expectations. In fact, prices in the stock market suggest a *market-implied forecast period* of between ten and fifteen years.

Of course, market-implied forecast periods for various industries can differ: In early 2001, for example, the market-implied forecast period for the personal computer hardware industry was shorter than ten years, whereas the period for the pharmaceutical industry exceeded twenty years. Furthermore, implied forecast periods for companies cluster within an industry, although these periods can change over time. In chapter 5, we will show precisely how to estimate the market-implied forecast period. The key thing to remember is that the stock market takes a long-term view.

FROM CORPORATE VALUE TO SHAREHOLDER VALUE

The present value of free cash flows for the forecast period plus the residual value equals corporate value. Shareholder value equals corporate value plus nonoperating assets minus debt.

You might wonder why we incorporate nonoperating assets—like excess cash, marketable securities, and other investments not essential to daily operations—in shareholder value. We do so because they have value and because we excluded the cash they will generate from the free cash-flow calculation. Excess cash is the cash over and above what a company needs for current operations. Companies sometimes stockpile cash and marketable securities to weather an industry downturn or to prepare for a large acquisition. Nonoperating assets can represent a significant percentage of a company's stock price. For example, in November 2000, cash and marketable securities accounted for between 30 and 56 percent of the stock price of AMR, Apple Computer, Bausch & Lomb, Delta Air Lines, Ford, and General Motors.[11] A company's cash requirements for its daily operations vary from industry to industry— from 1 percent of sales for stable businesses such as packaged goods to 4 percent for volatile businesses such as biotechnology.[12]

Finally, we subtract the market value of debt to obtain shareholder value. Debt includes not only bonds but also preferred stock, employee stock options, and underfunded pension plans.[13] We deduct the value of preferred stock because a company must ordinarily pay preferred dividends in full before it can distribute cash to its common shareholders. We deduct employee stock options because they constitute a significant cost of doing business, and failure to deduct the liability for options granted but unexercised overstates shareholder value. (See chapter 5 for how to value employee stock options.) The pension plan liability is deducted when the present value of projected pension benefit obligations is greater than plan assets. Because sponsoring companies are ultimately responsible for the underfunding, you should deduct the underfunded balance to determine shareholder value.[14]

SUMMARY ILLUSTRATION

To calculate shareholder value in the following example, we start with operating value driver assumptions and end with shareholder value. The expectations investing process operates in reverse: It starts with market value and solves for the price-implied expectations. The mechanics are the same going in either direction.

Assume that last year's sales were $100 million and that you expect the following value drivers to be constant over an entire five-year forecast period:

Sales growth rate	12%
Operating profit margin	10%

Cash tax rate	35%
Incremental fixed-capital rate	10%
Working-capital investment rate	5%
Cost of capital	10%

Assume that the company has no nonoperating assets or debt.

	Year 1	Year 2	Year 3	Year 4	Year 5
Sales	$112.00	$125.44	$140.49	$157.35	$176.23
Operating profit	11.20	12.54	14.05	15.74	17.63
Less: Cash taxes on operating profit	3.92	4.39	4.92	5.51	6.17
Net operating profit after tax (NOPAT)	7.28	8.15	9.13	10.23	11.46
Incremental fixed-capital investment	1.20	1.34	1.51	1.69	1.89
Working-capital investment	0.60	0.67	0.75	0.84	0.94
	1.80	2.02	2.26	2.53	2.83
Free cash flow	5.48	6.14	6.87	7.70	8.62
Present value of free cash flow	4.98	5.07	5.16	5.26	5.35
Cumulative present value of free cash flow	4.98	10.05	15.22	20.48	**25.83**
Present value of residual value					**90.69**
Shareholder value					**$116.52**

Shareholder value is the sum of the $25.83 million cumulative present value of free cash flow and the $90.69 million present value of residual value.[15]

ESSENTIAL IDEAS

- The magnitude, timing, and riskiness of cash flows determine the market prices of financial assets, including bonds, real estate, and stocks.

- You can estimate the value of a stock—its shareholder value—by forecasting free cash flows and discounting them back to the present.

- Rather than struggle to forecast long-term cash flows or employ unreliable, short-term valuation proxies, expectations investors establish the future cash-flow performance implied by stock prices as a benchmark for deciding whether to buy, hold, or sell.

Appendix: Estimating Residual Value

You can estimate residual value by using either the *perpetuity method* or the *perpetuity-with-inflation method*. The latter method works better for a vast majority of companies.

THE PERPETUITY METHOD

The perpetuity method assumes that a company generating returns greater than its cost of capital will attract competition that will, by the end of the forecast period, drive returns on new investments down to the cost of capital. It assumes that even if a company continues to grow beyond the forecast period, it will earn only the cost of capital rate on its investments and will therefore create no further value after the forecast period. To capture this dynamic, you can treat all post-forecast cash flows as a perpetuity, that is, an infinite stream of identical cash flows. This treatment greatly simplifies the calculation because we needn't discount individual cash flows.[16]

To determine the present value of a perpetuity, simply divide the expected annual cash flow by the rate of return:

EQUATION 2-5

$$\text{Present value of a perpetuity} = \frac{\text{Annual cash flow}}{\text{Rate of return}}$$

Using the perpetuity method, we calculate present value (at the end of the forecast period) by dividing NOPAT—or free cash flow *before* incremental investment—by the cost of capital:

EQUATION 2-6

$$\text{Perpetuity residual value} = \frac{\text{NOPAT}}{\text{Cost of capital}}$$

NOPAT, not free cash flow, is the correct perpetuity because the present value of the incremental investment outlays exactly offsets the expected present value of the incremental cash inflows. As a result, we need not consider these investments in the post-forecast period.

Since investments in the post-forecast period do not affect value, the residual value calculation has to account only for enough investment to maintain existing capacity. The perpetuity method assumes that the cost of maintaining existing capacity approximately equals the depreciation expense. That is why NOPAT is the numerator in equation 2-6.

THE PERPETUITY-WITH-INFLATION METHOD

Unlike the perpetuity method, the perpetuity-with-inflation approach assumes that the perpetuity will grow annually at the inflation rate in the post-forecast period. The formula for the present value (at the end of the forecast period) is an algebraic simplification of a growing perpetuity.

EQUATION 2-7

$$\text{Perpetuity with inflation} = \frac{\text{NOPAT} \times (1 + \text{Inflation rate})}{\text{Cost of capital} - \text{Inflation rate}}$$

How do these two methods differ? In both approaches the cost of capital (in the denominator) includes expected inflation. However, the cash flow in the numerator of the perpetuity model provides for no increases owing to inflation. Future cash flows are constant in nominal terms but decrease each year in real terms—that is, adjusted for inflation. In contrast, cash flows in the perpetuity-with-inflation model grow each year at the anticipated inflation rate. They are therefore constant in real terms. Predictably, when we anticipate inflation, the perpetuity-with-inflation model produces higher values than does the perpetuity model.

To illustrate, let's say that the cost of capital is 10 percent; the expected inflation, 2 percent; and NOPAT for the last year of the forecast period, $1.00. The residual value using the perpetuity method (equation 2-6) is simply the $1.00 NOPAT divided by the 10 percent cost of capital, or $10.00. In the perpetuity-with-inflation method (equation 2-7), NOPAT increases by the inflation rate, to $1.02. Divide $1.02 by 8 percent (10 percent cost of capital minus 2 percent expected inflation) to yield a residual value of $12.75.[17]

Which model is right for you? If you expect a company to keep up with inflation in the post-forecast period, you should use the perpetuity-with-inflation method. The case for this approach is strongest for well-positioned companies in sectors with compelling long-term growth prospects.

3
the expectations
infrastructure

Expectations investing rests on two simple ideas: First, you can read stock prices and estimate the expectations that they imply. Second, you will earn superior returns only if you correctly anticipate *revisions* in those price-implied expectations.

The market values stocks using the discounted cash-flow model, and so we'll use it to read expectations. The familiar operating value drivers—sales growth, operating profit margin, and investment—express price-implied expectations.

But now we turn our attention to expectations *revisions*. In this chapter, we deal with two fundamental questions:

1. Where should we look for expectations revisions?

2. Are all expectations revisions created equal?

The answers are vital because they hold the key to earning superior investment returns. Knowing today's expectations is one thing, but knowing what they'll be and the impact they'll have on shareholder value is another thing altogether. Let's start by answering the first question.

THE EXPECTATIONS INFRASTRUCTURE

The operating value drivers are a logical place to start the search for expectations revisions. Indeed, investors and managers typically create ranges around each of the value drivers to test how they affect shareholder value. We too advocated this method until we realized that this sensitivity analysis doesn't truly capture the underpinnings of expectations revisions.

To see why, take a simple example. Let's say that the price-implied expectation for a company's operating profit margin is 10 percent. A sensitivity analysis substitutes a range of margins—9 to 11 percent, for instance—for the 10 percent, and measures the impact on shareholder value. But any change in the operating margin assumption raises a larger question: *Why* will margins change from current expectations? Will a change in sales growth expectations precipitate it? Or will the company modify its cost structure more aggressively than investors currently contemplate? Since value drivers change for many reasons, we know there is more to the story.

To understand expectations revisions, we must realize that changes in operating value drivers are really the culminating *effect*, not the fundamental *cause*, of expectations revisions. As it turns out, the right place to start anticipating expectations revisions is with the fundamental building blocks of shareholder value: sales, operating costs, and investments. Given that these fundamentals start the expectations revisions process, we call these building blocks *value triggers*. Importantly, investors and managers think and talk in precisely these terms.

But the value triggers are too broad to be mapped directly to the operating value drivers. For example, an increase in a company's expected sales may or may not affect operating profit margins. So to track the relationship between the value triggers and the value drivers systematically, we need one more set of analytical tools: the *value factors*. Value factors include volume, price and mix, operating leverage, economies of scale, cost efficiencies, and investment efficiencies.

Value triggers, value factors, and operating value drivers constitute the *expectations infrastructure* (figure 3-1). We now know where to begin to look for revisions in expectations: the value triggers. Once we've identified a potential change, we consider which value factors come into play. Finally, we can translate the revisions into value driver terms and calculate their impact on shareholder value.

The expectations infrastructure, while based on well-established microeconomic principles, is a potent new tool that enables investors to analyze historical and prospective performance rigorously. In addition, the expectations infrastructure sorts out cause and effect, providing investors with a clear-cut means to evaluate all the factors that come into play with a trigger revision. Wall Street's widely used tools simply do not capture this analysis of cause and effect.

Now let's go to the core of the expectations infrastructure and discuss each of the value factors.

FIGURE 3-1   The Expectations Infrastructure

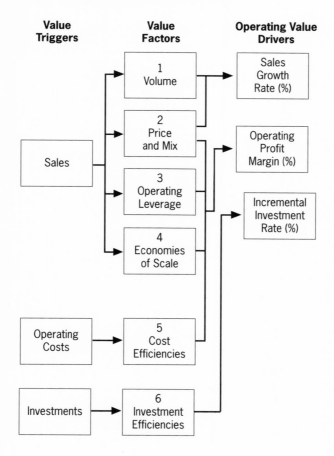

Value Factor 1: Volume

Changes in volume, price, and sales mix assumptions lead to revisions in sales growth expectations. Specifically, volume captures the expectations revisions for the number of units sold. Volume changes clearly induce sales changes and may also affect operating profit margins. Since we capture these margin effects via two additional factors—operating leverage and economies of scale—we need to focus only on the sales impact here.

Value Factor 2: Price and Mix

Changes in selling prices and sales mix affect both the sales growth rate and the operating profit margin. A change in selling price means that a company sells the same unit at a different price, whereas sales mix reflects a change in the distribution of high- and low-margin products.

For an example of how sales mix can materially affect operating profit margins, let's look at Ford Motor Company. In 1999 Ford earned more than any other auto manufacturer in history, even though its U.S. market share declined from 25.7 percent in 1995 to 23.8 percent in 1999. The key was sales mix: Ford posted a 600,000-unit increase in high-margin vehicles and a 42,000-unit decrease in low-margin vehicle sales in the period. Even though Ford reduced prices for its most profitable vehicles to boost demand, its operating profit margins still increased.[1]

Value Factor 3: Operating Leverage

Businesses invariably spend significant amounts of money before their products and services generate sales. We call these outlays *preproduction costs*. Some businesses, like utilities and chemical companies, spend primarily on physical facilities and equipment that they expense, via depreciation, over the estimated useful lives of these assets. Other businesses, including software and pharmaceutical companies, immediately expense their significant knowledge development costs but don't spend much on depreciable assets. The relative significance of preproduction costs and the time required to develop products or services varies across industries and companies.

Preproduction outlays dampen operating profit margins. Subsequent sales growth, on the other hand, leads to higher operating profit margins. Investors and managers commonly call this margin-increasing phenomenon *operating leverage.*

What determines the timing and magnitude of preproduction costs? As physical-capital-based companies approach practical capacity utilization, they need a new round of preproduction costs to sustain growth. These new costs pressure margins. In contrast, knowledge companies worry relatively little about their physical capacity. But to avoid obsolescence, they must incur successive rounds of product development costs in order to upgrade existing products and introduce new products.

So how exactly does operating leverage affect operating profit margin? Assume that a company had sales of $100 million and pretax operating profit of $10 million in the most recent year. Of the $90 million in operating costs, preproduction costs accounted for 20 percent, or $18 million. Because the company completed a major expansion last year, preproduction costs remain flat over the next two years while other operating costs continue at 72 percent of sales.

We can use these assumptions to calculate pretax operating profit for the first two forecast years.

	Year 0	Year 1	Year 2
Sales	$ 100.00	$ 112.00	$ 125.44
Preproduction costs	18.00	18.00	18.00
Other operating costs (72% of sales)	72.00	80.64	90.32
Total operating costs	90.00	98.64	108.32
Operating profit	$ 10.00	$ 13.36	$ 17.12
Operating profit margin	10.00%	11.93%	13.65%

Operating leverage increases pretax operating profit margin from 10 percent in the base year to 11.93 percent and 13.65 percent in years 1 and 2, respectively.

Value Factor 4: Economies of Scale

Economies of scale exist when a business can perform key tasks—purchasing, production, marketing, sales, distribution, customer services—at a lower cost per unit as volume increases.

For example, large-volume purchasers such as The Home Depot, General Motors, and McDonald's use their bargaining power to obtain favorable prices from their suppliers. Large companies also enjoy economies of scale in advertising because higher volume enables them not only to negotiate lower prices but also to reach more potential customers. These economies give larger companies a cost advantage over smaller competitors; if large enough, they can deter new competitors from entering the marketplace.

But the simple pursuit of market share and scale is no panacea, as Adrian Slywotzky and Joao Baptista warn. For example, Southwest Airlines and steel producer Nucor developed superior business models and became more profitable than their much larger competitors.[2]

Also, volume-driven companies may struggle to change course with the market in industries with rapid technological change and shifting customer demands. Too often, market leaders fall prey not only to costly bureaucracy but also to hubris. Bigger is not always better. If it is better, then it is not forever.

Investors should tread cautiously before betting on *long-term* increases in economies of scale. If economies of scale were unlimited, then one or two companies would dominate each industry.

How do economies of scale differ from operating leverage?[3] Whereas operating leverage is the result of spreading preproduction costs over larger volumes, economies of scale generate greater efficiency as volumes increase. Mistaking operating leverage for economies of scale may lead you to falsely conclude that a company's unit costs will continue to fall even as it expands capacity to meet demand.

How important are economies of scale to expectations investors? The answer depends not on the magnitude of a company's past scale economies, but rather on the extent to which the market's current expectations do *not* reflect plausible changes.[4]

Value Factor 5: Cost Efficiencies

Cost efficiencies, which are *unrelated to scale*, can also affect operating profit margin. These efficiencies span activities from raw-material acquisition to the sale and distribution of goods or services. Companies achieve cost efficiencies in two fundamental ways.[5] Either they reduce costs within activities, or they significantly reconfigure their activities.

General Electric is a good example of a company that enjoys cost efficiencies. It began its well-publicized Six Sigma error-reduction initiative in 1996 to improve efficiency in all its internal operations—from the factory floor to the backrooms of financial services. According to the company, the program "has flourished to the point where it has produced more than $2 billion in benefits in 1999, with much more to come this decade."[6]

Reconfiguring purchasing, production, sales, marketing, or distribution activities can dramatically shift cost position. Dell Computer's experience is a case in point. Traditionally, personal computer (PC) manufacturers sold primarily through distributors, resellers, and retail outlets. Dell recognized that both businesses and individual consumers seek low prices and customized PCs. It responded by selling customized PCs directly to the customer, effectively cutting sales force and distribution costs. Dell also pioneered PC assemblage to replace manufacturing. The company purchases components from a network of suppliers just in time, assembles them, and carries virtually no inventory. Further cost efficiencies will materialize as customers conduct more business on Dell's Web site. Here again, the focus should not be on the size of cost savings, but on the savings potential beyond the market's current expectations.

Value Factor 6: Investment Efficiencies

Businesses enjoy investment efficiencies when they can invest less for a given level of sales and operating profit.[7] For example, McDonald's continues to grow by opening new stores. The company has figured out a way to minimize new store investment—for the building itself, for the land, and for the equipment. For example, in 1990, the average cost for a traditional McDonald's restaurant was $1.6 million. By 1994, McDonald's had trimmed the cost to $1.1 million, a 30 percent reduction, by simplifying the building design and using modular buildings, which require smaller land parcels. The company also standardized its equipment, which allowed it to source globally and to demand lower prices from its main suppliers.

Retailing giant Wal-Mart benefits from another investment efficiency, an improving cash conversion cycle. During fiscal 2000, Wal-
Mart announced its objective "to sell merchandise before we pay for it."[8]
At the time, Wal-Mart sold roughly 63 percent of its inventory before
paying its bills. The company expected to sell its entire inventory before
paying its suppliers by the end of fiscal 2003. Given Wal-Mart's massive
size, this initiative could reduce working capital by more than $3 billion
and reduce future incremental working capital needs as well.

NOT ALL EXPECTATIONS REVISIONS ARE EQUAL

The expectations infrastructure provides a detailed map of what's
behind the three operating value drivers. It also shows why we need to
start with the value triggers to maximize our chances of successfully
anticipating revisions in expectations. But we still have to answer our
prior query—are all expectations revisions created equal? The answer is
an unequivocal no. To see why, we consider two related questions:

1. Which expectations changes—sales, costs, or investments—are
   likely to offer investors the best opportunities?

2. When do these changes really matter?

The first question has a clear-cut answer: Changes in sales expectations are the most likely to present attractive investment opportunities.
Why? Take another look at the expectations infrastructure (figure 3-1).
Note that sales trigger four of the six value factors. That argument is
compelling enough, but we also need to consider that the sales growth
rate typically has the largest revisions in expectations. Revisions in
expectations due to cost and investment efficiencies are almost always
smaller. But even the magnitude of the value driver shifts does not tell
the whole story, because our primary interest is the impact on shareholder value.

So when do shifts in sales growth expectations really matter? That
depends on whether a company is creating shareholder value, that is,
whether a company generates returns on its growth investments that
exceed its cost of capital. If a company earns exactly the cost of capital,
growth adds no value. Likewise, if returns fall below the cost of capital,

then growth destroys value. Growth can be good news, bad news, or no news.

A company adds value when the present value of incremental net operating profit after tax (NOPAT) exceeds incremental investment. NOPAT growth, in turn, depends on an expected sales growth rate, an operating profit margin, and an assumed cash tax rate. So, for a given change in sales growth expectations, the operating profit margin determines the impact on shareholder value added.[9] Obviously, the higher the margin, the better. However, just to maintain its value, a company needs to earn a certain break-even operating profit margin, which we call the *threshold margin*.[10]

To illustrate the threshold margin, we return to the summary illustration from chapter 2. Last year's sales were $100 million, and NOPAT was $6.50. Let's assume a one-year forecast period with market expectations as follows:

Sales growth rate	12%
Operating profit margin	10%
Cash tax rate	35%
Incremental investment rate	15%

The company's cost of capital is 10 percent, and the expected inflation rate is 2 percent (see equation 2–7). We calculate the shareholder value added for this set of assumptions in the "10 percent margin" column in table 3-1. In the next column, we substitute the 9.29 percent threshold margin for the 10 percent operating profit margin.[11] As a result, shareholder value added drops to zero.

The threshold margin draws out four guiding principles that can help you determine when expectations changes affect shareholder value:

1. If operating profit margin expectations are well above the threshold margin, then positive revisions in sales growth expectations produce large increases in shareholder value. The larger the revisions, the larger the increases.

2. If operating profit margin expectations are close to threshold margin, then revisions in sales growth expectations produce relatively small changes in shareholder value unless the revisions also induce

significant expectations revisions in sales mix, operating leverage, or economies of scale.

3. If operating profit margin expectations are significantly below the threshold margin, then positive revisions in sales growth expectations reduce shareholder value unless there are offsetting improvements in operating profit margin or investment rate expectations.

4. A rise in expectations in the incremental investment rate increases the threshold margin and thereby reduces the value that sales growth adds.

The wider the expected spread between operating profit margin and threshold margin and the faster the sales growth rate, the more likely that sales is the dominant trigger. When changes in sales also trigger the other value factors—price and mix, operating leverage, and economies of scale—the likelihood rises even more.

When do cost or investment value triggers dominate? For companies that earn returns close to the cost of capital and don't benefit much from price and mix, operating leverage, or changes in economies-of-scale expectations, revisions in sales expectations are insignificant. In these cases, changes in cost or investment efficiency can contribute

---

TABLE 3-1   Shareholder Value Added: Expectations versus Threshold Margin

	Year 0	Operating Profit Margin of 10%, Year 1	Threshold Margin of 9.29%, Year 1
Sales	$100.00	$112.00	$112.00
Operating profit	10.00	11.20	10.40
Less: Cash taxes on operating profit	3.50	3.92	3.64
Net operating profit after tax (NOPAT)	6.50	7.28	6.76
Less: Incremental investment		1.80	1.80
Free cash flow		5.48	4.96
Present value of free cash flow		4.98	4.51
Present value of residual value	82.88	84.38	78.37
Shareholder value	$ 82.88	$ 89.36	$ 82.88
Shareholder value added		**$ 6.48**	**$ 0.00**

most to changes in shareholder value (although the *absolute* impact on shareholder value may be small).

When expectations change, the expectations infrastructure helps you identify the potential sources of shareholder value added. The value triggers linked to the six value factors and the resulting operating value drivers are the analytical foundation for expectations investing analysis (see chapters 5 through 7).

In the next chapter, the final chapter of part I, we address the larger competitive issues that affect the fundamental value triggers. With the last piece in place, you will have all the strategic and financial tools you need to implement expectations investing.

ESSENTIAL IDEAS

- To earn superior returns, you must improve your odds of correctly anticipating revisions in market expectations.

- The expectations infrastructure—which stems from the fundamental value triggers, value factors, and operating value drivers that determine shareholder value—should help you visualize the causes and the effects of expectations revisions.

- Revisions in sales growth expectations are your most likely source of investment opportunities, but only when a company earns above the cost of capital on its investments.

4 analyzing
competitive
strategy

Competitive strategy analysis lies at the heart of security analysis. The surest way for investors to anticipate expectations revisions is to foresee shifts in a company's competitive dynamics. These shifts lead to a revised outlook for sales, costs, or investments—the value triggers—and initiate the expectations investing process. For investors, competitive strategy analysis is an essential tool in the expectations game.

THE DUAL USES OF
COMPETITIVE STRATEGY ANALYSIS

The competitive strategy literature focuses largely on prescriptions for management action. But investors can use the same strategic tools, albeit in a different way.

Management's objective is to create value by investing at above the cost of capital. Indeed, sustainable value creation is the signature of competitive advantage. And since a company's competitive advantage hinges squarely on the quality and execution of its strategies, competitive strategy analysis is vital to planning and decision making.

Investors play a very different game. They generate superior returns when they correctly anticipate *revisions* in market expectations for a company's performance. Investors do not earn superior rates of return on stocks that are priced to fully reflect future performance—even for the best value-creating companies—which is why great companies are not necessarily great stocks. Investors use competitive strategy analysis as a means to foresee expectations revisions.

HISTORICAL ANALYSIS

Looking at a company's historical results can help you as an investor know what to anticipate. For one thing, you can see which operating value drivers have been most variable. You can then analyze this information, using the expectations infrastructure and competitive strategy analysis, to track the forces behind the variability. For another thing, history provides a reality check. If the market expects a specific operating value driver to perform as it has in the past, you must have a good reason to believe that an expectations revision is likely.

The powerful combination of the expectations infrastructure and competitive strategy analysis highlights the economic and strategic factors that influence the operating value drivers. For example, a company may pass cost savings on to its customers through lower prices to try to accelerate unit volume growth. So even though lower prices offset the margin benefit of cost savings, price cuts are important because they drive sales growth. The expectations infrastructure provides a framework to assess cause and effect, whereas competitive strategy analysis goes beyond the numbers to assess a company's competitive circumstances. Figure 4-1 presents some key issues (along with the operating value drivers and value factors) that you may want to consider when you evaluate historical results.

Naturally, the relevance of historical analysis varies from company to company. Its relative importance is largely a function of the *availability of historical data* and *industry stability*. Generally speaking, the more historical data available, the better. A long string of past results provides important insights about previous industry cycles, competitive clashes, and the effectiveness of management strategies.

Industry stability speaks to the reliability of historical value drivers. For stable industries, for which the future will likely look a great deal like the past, a record of historical performance is invaluable. In contrast, looking at the past performance of rapidly changing sectors or companies that compete in brand-new industries has limited practical value.

COMPETITIVE STRATEGY FRAMEWORKS

You can conduct competitive strategy analysis by looking at industry attractiveness and a company's chosen strategies. *Industry attractiveness* has two prime determinants: market characteristics and industry structure. Market characteristics include growth in the market, supply and demand fundamentals (for both customers and suppliers), rate of innovation, and regulatory shifts. Industry structure involves market share, entry and exit barriers, vertical-integration potential, threat of substitute products, modes of competition, and industry profitability.

FIGURE 4-1   Operating Value Drivers, Value Factors, and Competitive Strategy Analysis

Operating Value Driver	Value Factor	Key Issues
Sales growth	Volume	• Industry growth • Market share
	Price and mix	• Price changes • Mix changes
Operating profit margin	Price and mix	• Price changes • Mix changes
	Operating leverage	• Preproduction costs • Position in investment cycle • Divisibility of investment
	Economies of scale	• Purchasing • Production • Distribution • Learning curve
	Cost efficiencies	• Process reconfiguration • Technology • Outsourcing
Incremental investment	Investment efficiencies	• Technology • Facilities reconfiguration • Working-capital management

An individual company generally has minimal influence over industry attractiveness. In contrast, the company's *chosen strategies*—for product quality, technology, vertical integration, cost position, service, pricing, brand identification, and distribution channel focus—drive its performance and competitive position. A company's strategic choices, in combination with its skills in executing them, determine its prospects for creating value.

We have identified four particularly useful frameworks for analyzing competitive strategy:

Framework	Strategic Issue
Five forces	Industry analysis
Value chain analysis	Choice of activities
Disruptive technology	Innovation
Information rules	Information economy

You probably don't need all four frameworks to analyze every company; two or three will generally give you enough insight to assess potential shifts in expectations. The goal is to match the company you're analyzing with the relevant frameworks.

Five Forces: Industry Analysis

Michael Porter's well-known five-forces framework, which helps define industry structure, is particularly useful for competitive analysis (figure 4-2).[1] Industry structure is a major force in shaping the competitive rules of the game as well as the strategies available to competing firms. This analysis is applicable to most industries, but especially to those with the following three characteristics:

- *Defined boundaries.* You can define buyers, suppliers, and competitors easily.

- *Mature and relatively predictable patterns.* The industry is relatively stable.

- *A physical-capital orientation.* Physical assets are central to value creation.

Porter argues that the collective strength of the five forces determines an industry's potential for value creation. He stresses that although this potential varies from industry to industry, an individual company's strategies ultimately dictate the company's sustainable competitive advantage. Let's look at the five forces one by one:

- *Barriers to entry* determine how difficult it is for a new competitor to enter an industry. These barriers might include the level of capital required to enter an industry, the strength of established brands and customer loyalty, access to distribution channels, economies of scale, the costs of switching from one supplier's product to another supplier's, and government regulations.

- *Substitution threat* addresses the existence of substitute products or services, as well as the likelihood that a potential buyer will switch to a substitute product. A business faces a substitution threat if its prices are not competitive and if comparable products are available from competitors. Substitute products limit the prices that companies can charge, placing a ceiling on potential returns.

FIGURE 4-2   The Five Forces That Define Industry Attractiveness

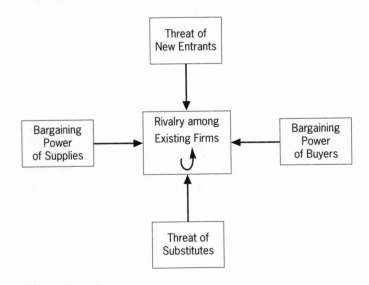

Source: Reprinted with the permission of The Free Press, a Division of Simon & Schuster, Inc., from *Competitive Strategy: Techniques for Analyzing Industries and Competitors* by Michael E. Porter. Copyright © 1980, 1998 by The Free Press.

- *Buyer power* is the bargaining strength of the buyers of a product or service. It is a function of buyer concentration, switching costs, levels of information, substitute products, and the offering's importance to the buyer. Informed, large buyers have much more leverage over their suppliers than do uninformed, diffused buyers.

- *Supplier power* is the degree of leverage a supplier has with its customers in areas like price, quality, and service. An industry that cannot pass on to its customers price increases from its powerful suppliers is destined to be unattractive. Suppliers are well positioned if they are more concentrated than the industry they sell to, if they are not burdened by substitute products, or if their products have significant switching costs. They are also in a good position if the industry they serve represents a relatively small percentage of their sales volume or if the product is critical to the buyer. Sellers of commodity goods to a concentrated number of buyers are in a much more difficult position than sellers of differentiated products to a diverse buyer base.

- *Rivalry among firms* addresses how fiercely companies compete with one another along dimensions such as price, service, warranties, new-product introductions, and advertising. Intense rivalry can make an industry unattractive for all participating companies. Factors that influence rivalry include industry growth, the relative size of preproduction costs, and the level of product differentiation. A growing industry tends to mitigate rivalry, as competitors often focus more on growing with the industry than on prevailing in zero-sum games. Industries with high preproduction costs usually exhibit significant rivalry, as there are acute incentives to drive sufficient volume to cover costs. Where little product differentiation exists, intense rivalry based on price and service frequently materializes.

Although we conduct five-forces analysis at the industry level, we ultimately want to understand potential expectations revisions for *individual companies*. Further, the five-forces framework paints a static picture. Therefore we must revisit the framework periodically to see how the competitive landscape has changed. Is the sector consolidating? What is happening to industry capacity? Are managers competing more or less rationally? These and other similar questions must be periodically addressed.

ANTICIPATING COMPETITOR MOVES

If you're thinking about building a new paper facility, you're going to base your decision on some assumptions about economic growth. . . . *What we never seem to factor in, however, is the response of our competitors. Who else is going to build a plant or machine at the same time?*
—CFO, International Paper (emphasis added)

You can't assess a company's actions in a void, because companies respond to each other's competitive moves. Game theory is a useful tool for thinking about industry rivalry and is particularly applicable in two business situations: pricing and capacity additions in a cyclical business.[a]

Industries that price their products cooperatively stand to garner greater industry profits, as shown by the late 1990s exchange between Kodak and Fuji in the film market. In 1997, Fuji cut prices and successfully gained market share. Kodak responded by dropping its prices the following year, nudging up its share. When the dust settled, each company's share was stable, but industry prices and profits were down. After this realization, the companies moved to a more cooperative, and profitable, stance in 1999.[b]

Another illustration is the decision to add capacity at a cyclical peak. If a company adds capacity and its competitors do not, it earns significant incremental profits. If it forgoes the investment and its competitors add the capacity, the competitors earn the incremental profits. If *all* the players add capacity, however, no one benefits and the next cyclical downturn is more painful for all. Thus the competitive reactions to a company's actions can have a material impact on expectations revisions.

[a]Adam M. Brandenburger and Barry J. Nalebuff, *Co-opetition: 1. A Revolutionary Mindset That Combines Competition and Cooperation. 2. The Game Theory Strategy That's Changing the Game of Business* (New York: Doubleday, 1996).

[b]Gibboney Huske, "Eastman Kodak Company: Film Pricing—A Prisoner's Dilemma," *Credit Suisse First Boston Equity Research*, 16 February 1999.

Value Chain Analysis: Choice of Activities

Michael Porter also has popularized value chain analysis, which views a business as a "collection of activities that are performed to design, produce, market, deliver and support its product."[2] He argues that you cannot understand competitive advantage by looking at the firm as a whole. Rather, you must analyze the discrete activities that a company performs to deliver its goods or services. Each activity contributes or detracts from a company's ability to capture and sustain competitive advantage.

Porter shows that you can analyze a company's cost position or product differentiation relative to its peers by disaggregating its strategically relevant activities. A comparison of value chains among companies within an industry helps you see the points of difference that determine competitive advantage.

Value chain analysis is relevant for most businesses, but especially those engaging in two key types of activities:

- *Vertically integrated activities.* Vertically integrated businesses engage in all the activities necessary to convert raw materials into a final product. Value chain analysis helps identify which activities a company performs relatively efficiently. This analysis is especially useful when a company can substantially improve or outsource low-return activities.

- *Activities susceptible to technological change.* Technology causes value chains to disintegrate, and allows companies to specialize in a narrow set of activities. Vertically integrated companies that rely on a handful of activities for their profitability are at risk from specialized companies that perform that activity better.

Adrian Slywotzky suggests starting the value chain analysis with the customer, which underscores that the world is becoming more and more customer centric and requires greater corporate responsiveness and flexibility than ever. In his view, the "modern value chain" comprises five activities: customer priorities, channels, offering, inputs/raw materials, and assets/core competencies (figure 4-3):[3]

- *Customer priorities.* Companies must continually define their customers' needs and priorities. If customer priorities shift, or if the customer group itself changes, then companies must shift the emphasis of their activities. For example, Clay Christensen and Matt Verlinden argue that as the performance of a product or service exceeds customer demands, customers shift their priorities away from product performance to lower prices and delivery flexibility. This in turn spurs a shift in the most valuable activities in the industry-wide value chain.[4]

- *Channels.* A company uses distribution channels to deliver its products or services to its customers. Technology is causing major changes in distribution. For example, look at how the Internet has affected the financial services industry. Merrill Lynch built a market-leading industry position by channeling its offering through an army of full-service stockbrokers. It charges high fees because it packages investment advice along with its trading capabilities. Charles Schwab & Co., on the other hand, launched its business by targeting savvy investors who require only trading capabilities. Schwab could price its service at a significant discount to the full-service brokers and thus was ideally positioned to significantly increase its market position by offering its services through a powerful new channel, the Internet.

- *Offering.* The objective is to identify and provide the most appropriate products and services to flow through the channels. A product or service offering should address customer priorities, including price and variety. A company must balance customer satisfaction against the cost of providing the good or service.

FIGURE 4-3   The Modern Value Chain

Source: From *The Profit Zone* by Adrian J. Slywotzky and David J. Morrison, copyright © 1997 by Mercer Management Consulting, Inc. Used by permission of Times Books, a division of Random House, Inc.

- *Inputs/raw materials.* This aspect of the value chain involves the raw materials, or inputs, that are necessary to deliver the products or services. Supplier management is becoming increasingly important. Strong supplier relationships lead to a virtual value chain, which allows a company to focus its energies on the activities that add the most value.

- *Assets/core competency.* A company's choice of activities dictates the assets it requires—physical or intangible—and its required core competency, that is, its collective know-how. For example, Nike has defined marketing as its core competency. So rather than invest in substantial manufacturing assets, it focuses its efforts on product design and consumer marketing. To create sustainable competitive advantage, a company's assets and competencies must support its various activities.

Adding another important facet to the value chain framework, Philip Evans and Thomas Wurster note that information links all the steps in a value chain: It is the glue that holds them together. Evans and Wurster also emphasize that the economic characteristics of information and of physical goods differ.[5]

The explosion in technology allows for a separation between information and physical goods, leaving some businesses—especially incumbents—potentially vulnerable. For example, an Internet-based retailer can offer substantial information content on the Web and still maintain lean physical inventories. So when a company can separate information and products, it can "deconstruct" the value chain. Slywotzky and his colleagues dub this division of activities "the great value chain split."[6]

Evans and Wurster cite the newspaper industry as a prime example of deconstruction.[7] The risk to the business is not electronic newspapers, or even the news customization that the leading Internet portals provide. The threat of deconstruction lies in the migration of classified advertising—the most profitable activity in the newspaper value chain—to the Internet. Without the benefit of classified advertising revenue, other supporting activities like content, printing, and distribution are unattractive.

Disruptive Technology: Innovation

Also useful to help you anticipate expectations changes is Clay Christensen's model of "disruptive technology."[8] The model exposes a pattern by which dominant companies can fail, leading to sharply lowered expectations. This framework is particularly relevant for the following types of companies:

- *Technology rich.* Many fast-moving businesses have trouble embracing the next technology wave.

- *Market leaders.* These companies listen to their customers and focus on current profits. As a result, they often miss significant technological shifts.

- *Organizationally centralized.* When companies centralize their decision making, they have difficulty seeing disruptive technologies emerge.

Christensen argues that many companies fail to retain their leadership positions even though great managers are making sound decisions based on widely accepted management principles. Hence the dilemma. His framework is based on three findings:

First, *sustaining* technologies and *disruptive* technologies are quite distinct. Sustaining technologies foster product improvement. They can be incremental, discontinuous, or even radical. But sustaining technologies operate within a defined value network—the "context within which a firm identifies and responds to customers' needs, solves problems, procures input, reacts to competitors, and strives for profit."[9] In direct contrast, disruptive technologies offer the market a very different value proposition. Products based on disruptive technologies may initially appeal only to relatively few customers who value features such as low price, smaller size, or greater convenience. Furthermore, Christensen finds that these technologies generally underperform established products in the near term. Thus, not surprisingly, leading companies often overlook, ignore, or dismiss disruptive technologies in the early phases of the technology.

Second, technologies often progress faster than the market demands. Established companies commonly provide customers with more than they need or more than they are ultimately willing to pay for. This allows disruptive technologies to emerge, because even if they underperform the demands of users today, they become fully performance-competitive tomorrow.

Finally, passing over disruptive technologies may appear rational for established companies, because disruptive products generally offer low margins, operate in insignificant or emerging markets, and are not in demand by the company's most profitable customers. As a result, companies that listen to their customers and practice conventional financial discipline are apt to pass on disruptive technologies.

Certainly, companies should *not* stop listening to their customers; doing so would be at odds with the customer-centric value chain. Rather, companies must both meet their customers' needs today and anticipate their needs for tomorrow. Sometimes, customers themselves don't know which products or services they will want. Given that disruptive technologies may provide tomorrow's customer solutions, companies must always balance what works now and what might work in the future, because today's solutions may quickly become obsolete. As Intel's Andy Grove puts it, "Only the paranoid survive."[10]

The retail book industry is an example of a disruptive technology in action.[11] At the time of Amazon.com's initial public offering (IPO) in May 1997, leading book retailers Barnes & Noble and Borders were significantly improving their standard bookselling business model by rolling out superstores. These stores offer unprecedented convenience, prices, assortment, service, and ambience—important sustaining technologies. In contrast, Amazon.com offers a different experience. It quickly improved the customer proposition along several important dimensions, including assortment, price, and convenience. Amazon didn't beat the traditional booksellers at their own game. It completely redefined the game and launched a new value network.

The Amazon strategy also created a massive shift in expectations—and hence market capitalizations. From its IPO to early 2001, Amazon's market capitalization rose by about $5 billion. During that same period, Barnes & Noble and Borders saw their combined market capitalizations shrink by some $400 million.

Disruptive technologies caused investors to lower expectations for some of the world's best-known companies, including Digital Equipment, Merrill Lynch, and IBM. They have also helped create new and valuable businesses, although business innovation and value creation are not always synonymous.[12] You should be alert for the emergence of new value networks and the seeds of expectations changes that they sow.

Information Rules: Information Economics

The final competitive strategy framework, information rules, concerns the nature and characteristics of information products, such as software, recorded music, and proprietary networks. The global economy is shifting from reliance on physical capital to reliance on intellectual, or knowledge, capital. Information rules, which economists Carl Shapiro and Hal Varian superbly articulate, apply to all knowledge businesses.[13]

Before we proceed, let us make one point clear: The laws of economics have not changed. As Shapiro and Varian convincingly show, basic economic principles are durable enough to explain the information economy. The key is that knowledge-based companies have characteristics distinct from physical-asset-based companies. As a result, you must evaluate them somewhat differently. Some of these characteristics include the following:

- *High up-front, low incremental costs.* Many knowledge products are very costly to create the first time. Once in digital form, however, they are relatively inexpensive to replicate and distribute. Take software. Microsoft spent about $2 billion to create the first Windows 2000 disk. But replicating and distributing that disk was extremely cheap. As a result, Microsoft has enjoyed "increasing returns."[14] Every incremental unit of a knowledge product that a company sells amortizes the fixed, up-front cost. Thus, knowledge-based companies enjoy increasing, not diminishing, returns. Nevertheless, the heightened pace of new innovation virtually assures that increasing returns are short-lived. In brief, the high up-front, low incremental costs of knowledge goods, coupled with technology-driven demand shifts, can lead to explosive, albeit often short-term, value creation.

- *Network effects.* Network effects exist when the value of a product or service increases as more members use that product. As an example, online auctioneer eBay is attractive to a user precisely because so many buyers and sellers congregate there. In a particular category, positive feedback typically assures that one network becomes dominant: eBay has not only weathered competitive onslaughts but strengthened its position. So as winner-take-all markets develop, variability increases as industry profits migrate to the dominant player. Expectations for the winner rise just as expectations for the losers deflate.

• *Lock-in.* Once customers develop user skills with a given product, or set corporate standards for a product, they often hesitate to switch to a competing offering, even if a rival product performs better. Hence, the company has "locked in" customers, making them more open to purchasing highly profitable product upgrades than they are to purchasing products from other sources. Shapiro and Varian cite multiple forms of lock-in, including brand-specific training and loyalty programs.[15]

When information companies enjoy these three advantages, they usually have developed certain related strategies. When you evaluate knowledge-based companies, be sure to investigate how they rely on the following:

• *Giveaways.* In spite of the heavy up-front costs of knowledge goods, a company's ability to establish a large user base as quickly as possible increases the potential of building a valuable network and locking in customers. Hence, giving away products (or heavily discounting them) in the short term is often the best way for a company to build long-term value.

The implicit understanding in the give-it-away strategy is that established users will be valuable to the company as a source of future revenues, through product upgrades, ancillary products, or marketing. One example is Hotmail, a free e-mail service. Hotmail garnered 1 million users within six months of its 1996 launch. After eighteen months, it was up to 12 million users and, by the summer of 2000, had over 45 million users. Each user fills out a detailed demographic profile, which contributes to a valuable database that attracts advertisers. Hotmail then sells advertising on its Web site. Microsoft validated Hotmail's give-it-away strategy by buying the company in 1997 for approximately $400 million.

- *Link-and-leverage.* You should also watch link-and-leverage, economist W. Brian Arthur's term for the transfer of a user base built on one node of technology to one built on neighboring nodes. Once customers become accustomed to a given technology or interface, link-and-leverage becomes a powerful way to create value. Microsoft's product evolution from operating systems, to applications, to Internet access is one example. Link-and-leverage highlights the value of real options, a topic we take up in chapter 8.

- *Adaptation.* Adaptation is more valuable than optimization. Many mature physical businesses are optimizers—they perpetually improve their processes to enhance value. Knowledge companies, on the other hand, must be alert for the next "big thing." Because products become obsolete so quickly, companies must continually seek new opportunities—often at the risk of cannibalizing their current, profitable businesses.

Without a doubt, variability is high for knowledge businesses. But a fundamental grasp of the prime characteristics of knowledge businesses can lead to important insights about potential expectations mismatches.

Expectations investing is not just about prospective changes in operating value drivers. It integrates the expectations infrastructure with competitive strategy analysis, helping the investor make informed judgments about where to find potentially profitable expectations.

ESSENTIAL IDEAS

- The surest path to anticipating shifts in expectations is to foresee shifts in a company's competitive dynamics.

- Management and investors have different performance hurdles. Management tries to achieve returns above the cost of capital. Investors try to anticipate changes in market expectations correctly.

• Historical performance provides insight into potential value driver variability by showing which operating value drivers have been most variable in the past. This type of analysis provides a reality check on expectations ranges.

• Four competitive strategy models can help investors better anticipate expectations changes: five forces, value chain, disruptive technology, and information rules.

• Although the laws of economics haven't changed, the characteristics of knowledge companies differ from those of physical companies.

Part II
implementing
the process

5 how to estimate price-implied expectations

As an investor, to earn superior investment returns, you must correctly anticipate the stock market's expectations revisions. But before you can consider the likelihood and magnitude of expectations revisions, you need to clearly understand where expectations stand today.

Ask an average group of investors if they are interested in reading market expectations, and you'll hear a resounding yes. But if you ask them how they go about reading the market, they'll probably fall back on a slew of contemporaneous, statistical benchmarks like short-term earnings and price-earnings multiples. Though ubiquitous, these investment shorthands aren't reliably linked to shareholder value, so they simply don't paint an economically sound picture of today's expectations.

To accurately read the expectations wrapped in stock prices, you must think in the market's terms. The long-term discounted cash-flow model best captures the stock market's pricing mechanism. Yet investors justifiably think forecasting distant cash flows is extraordinarily hazardous. Credible long-term forecasts are difficult to make, and they often serve only to reveal the forecasting investor's underlying biases. As

Warren Buffett says, "Forecasts usually tell us more of the forecaster than of the future."[1] Where, then, do you turn?

The ideal solution allows you to retain the discounted cash-flow model but frees you from the burden of cash-flow forecasts—which is precisely what expectations investing does. Instead of forecasting cash flows, expectations investing starts with the current stock price and uses the discounted cash-flow model to "read" what the market implies about a company's future performance. This estimate of *price-implied expectations* (PIE) launches the expectations investing process (figure 5-1).

Think about it this way: It's hard for an individual to forecast an uncertain future better than the collective wisdom of the market can. So why not get the "answer" about the PIE directly from the source?

Many investors (and managers) view stock prices with some misgiving, thinking that prices don't always accurately convey value. But expectations investors take a very different view. For them, stock price is the best and least-exploited information source available. Stock price— the dollar level at which buyers and sellers are willing to transact—most clearly and reliably indicates the market's expectations at any given time. You just need to know how to read the market *today*—and anticipate what the expectations are likely to be *tomorrow*.

One final thought before we explain how to read expectations. We have conducted expectations analysis on many stocks in our roles as teachers, security analysts, and consultants. The results typically surprise investors and corporate managers.

Investors who assume that the market focuses on the short term are amazed to find that it actually takes a long-term view. Corporate managers, who instinctively believe that the market undervalues their stock, are often startled to find that the market's expectations are more ambitious than their own. So prepare yourself: The results may surprise you the first few times you read PIE.

FIGURE 5-1   Expectations Investing Process

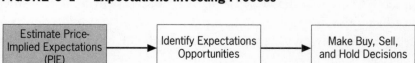

READING EXPECTATIONS

In chapter 2, we showed that a combination of free cash flows, the cost of capital, and a forecast period determines value in a discounted cash-flow model. We also noted that expectations investing uses the same computational tools but reverses the process: It starts with stock price (as distinct from value) and then estimates the expectations for cash flow, the cost of capital, and the forecast horizon.

We offer here some operational guidelines on how to read expectations. Although you should find these tips useful, be aware that reading expectations is as much an art as it is a science. The ability to read expectations improves with experience and industry knowledge.

Finally, you should go into this step of the expectations investing process without any preconceived notions. Try to be agnostic about the outcomes for now.

Cash Flows

You can consult a number of sources—Value Line Investment Survey, Standard & Poor's, Wall Street reports (available directly or via services like Multex.com), and other research services—to establish a market consensus forecast for operating value drivers, that is, sales growth rate, operating profit margin, and incremental investment rate. L.E.K. Consulting, which has conducted expectations analysis for scores of companies, provides some additional thoughts:[2]

- Determine consensus forecasts for sales growth, profits, and free cash flow. Consensus-tracking services such as First Call Corporation, I/B/E/S International, and Zacks Investment Research can help determine the general direction of expectations, even though they largely dwell on earnings.

- Assess information that management provides to investors. When management credibility is low, market expectations are often lower than management's publicly stated targets. When management credibility is high, expectations often exceed management's stated goals.

- Evaluate the industry environment, and consider whether the value driver expectations are reasonable in light of competitive circumstances.

- Review historical value driver performance, and note any meaningful differences between past and expected performance.

Cost of Capital

Use the approach outlined in chapter 2 to estimate a company's weighted average cost of capital. Here is some additional guidance:[3]

- Ibbotson.com is one of several services that estimate the cost of capital.

- Betas are available from multiple sources, including Value Line, Standard & Poor's, Barra.com, and Yahoo! Finance.

- Forward-looking market-risk premium estimates are available from various brokerage firms and advisory firms (e.g., Alcar.com).

Nonoperating Assets and Debt

You do not have to estimate most nonoperating assets or corporate liabilities like debt or underfunded pension funds, because they either appear on the balance sheet or are readily estimable. But you must deal with one corporate liability not on the balance sheet—employee stock options (ESOs). Given the recent surge in ESOs, this contingent liability is more meaningful than ever. In fact, you will find it very difficult to capture market expectations accurately, especially for young, knowledge-oriented companies, without incorporating past and future ESO grants.

You can estimate how ESOs affect value in two steps. First, value the already-granted ESOs and treat them as debt. Second, estimate future option grants and treat them as an expense (hence lowering future operating profit margins). The appendix at the end of this chapter shows you how to analyze this in detail, and provides a case study on Microsoft.

Market-Implied Forecast Period

The final value determinant is the number of years of free cash flows required to justify the stock price. We call this horizon the *market-implied forecast period* (it's also called "value growth duration" and "competitive advantage period").[4]

Practically, the market-implied forecast period measures how long the market expects a company to generate returns that exceed its cost of capital. The model assumes that, thereafter, investments earn the cost of capital and consequently add no further value. The market-implied forecast period for U.S. stocks clusters between ten and fifteen years, but it can range from zero to as long as thirty years for companies with strong competitive positions.

How do you estimate the market-implied forecast period? You've determined the market's expectations for future free cash flows and the cost of capital. To find the market-implied forecast period, extend the forecast horizon in the discounted cash-flow model as many years as it takes to arrive at today's price. For example, if you must extend your discounted free cash flows (plus residual value) twelve years to reach a company's current stock price, the market-implied forecast period is twelve years.

GATEWAY CASE STUDY

Gateway manufactures and markets a product line of personal computers directly to businesses, individuals, government agencies, and educational institutions. When we analyzed the company in April 2000, Gateway's 321 million shares outstanding traded at $52 each, for a market capitalization approaching $17 billion.

Cash Flows

To estimate the expectations that the $52 price implied, we reviewed both Value Line and analyst forecasts and surveyed leading analysts. We reached the following consensus forecast:

Sales growth rate	20.0%
Operating profit margin	9.0%
Cash tax rate	35.0%
Incremental fixed-capital rate	11.0%
Incremental working-capital rate	−5.0%

The sales growth rate, operating profit margin, and cash tax rate determine net operating profit after tax (NOPAT). Incremental fixed-capital and working-capital rates tell us that for every incremental dollar of sales, Gateway will invest $0.11 in fixed capital (capital expenditures less depreciation) and will *generate* $0.05 by reducing its working capital. Note that this is our best estimate of the *market's* view of Gateway's expected operating value driver performance.

Cost of Capital

At the time of the analysis, the yield on the risk-free ten-year treasury bond was 5.85 percent, the market risk premium estimate was 3.2 percent, and beta was 1.30, according to Value Line. Gateway was essentially 100 percent equity financed. So its cost of capital was equal to its cost of equity of 10 percent [5.85% + (3.20% × 1.30) = 10%].

Nonoperating Assets and Debt

At the end of 1999, Gateway had nonoperating assets consisting of excess cash and marketable securities of about $1.3 billion, or approximately $4.00 per share. Gateway's liabilities, almost exclusively employee stock options, totaled roughly $715 million, or $2.25 per share.

Market-Implied Forecast Period

Here is how we calculated Gateway's market-implied forecast period of seven years. Starting in year 2000, we calculate Gateway's shareholder value per share at the end of each year (table 5-1). We then extend the forecast period as far as necessary to match the current stock price. Our residual value is a perpetuity with inflation and assumes a 2 percent inflation rate.

We estimate Gateway's value at the end of 2000 to be $25.26 per

TABLE 5-1 Calculation of Market-Implied Forecast Period for Gateway (in millions)

	1999	2000	2001	2002	2003	2004	2005	2006
Sales	$8,645.56	$10,374.67	$12,449.61	$14,939.53	$17,927.44	$21,512.92	$25,815.51	$30,978.61
Operating profit	595.67	933.72	1,120.46	1,344.56	1,613.47	1,936.16	2,323.40	2,788.07
Less: Cash taxes on operating profit	208.48	326.80	392.16	470.60	564.71	677.66	813.19	975.83
Net operating profit after tax (NOPAT)	387.19	606.92	728.30	873.96	1,048.75	1,258.51	1,510.21	1,812.25
Incremental fixed-capital investment		190.20	228.24	273.89	328.67	394.40	473.28	567.94
Incremental working-capital investment		(86.46)	(103.75)	(124.50)	(149.40)	(179.27)	(215.13)	(258.16)
		103.75	124.50	149.40	179.27	215.13	258.16	309.79
Free cash flow		503.17	603.81	724.57	869.48	1,043.38	1,252.05	1,502.46
Present value of free cash flow		457.43	499.01	544.38	593.87	647.85	706.75	771.00
Cumulative value of residual value		457.43	956.44	1,500.82	2,094.69	2,742.54	3,449.29	4,220.29
Present value of residual value		7,034.74	7,674.26	8,371.92	9,133.00	9,963.27	10,869.03	11,857.12
Corporate value		$ 7,492.16	$ 8,630.70	$ 9,872.74	$11,227.69	$12,705.81	$14,318.32	$16,077.41
Add: Nonoperating assets		1,336.37	1,336.37	1,336.37	1,336.37	1,336.37	1,336.37	1,336.37
Less: Debt and other liabilities		(716.26)	(716.26)	(716.26)	(716.26)	(716.26)	(716.26)	(716.26)
Shareholder value		$ 8,112.28	$ 9,250.81	$10,492.85	$11,847.80	$13,325.93	$14,938.43	$16,697.52
Shareholder value per share		**$ 25.26**	**$ 28.80**	**$ 32.67**	**$ 36.89**	**$ 41.49**	**$ 46.51**	**$ 52.00**

share, and it increases each year until it reaches its $52 stock price at the end of 2006, the seventh year. The market-implied forecast period is therefore seven years.

WHY REVISIT EXPECTATIONS?

So when should you revisit PIE? You should do so either when stock prices change significantly or when a company discloses important new information. Frequently, both happen at the same time.

For example, companies that experience relatively large stock-price responses to earnings surprises are logical candidates for a fresh look at expectations analysis. Earnings surprises, favorable and unfavorable, sometimes lead to a market overreaction.

Consider the June 2000 announcement by Electronic Data Systems Corporation (EDS). Even though EDS expected to meet Wall Street earnings estimates for the second quarter and full year, it warned that its second-quarter sales growth would be well below the consensus expectations. Notwithstanding that EDS attributed the slowdown to "temporary softening," the market's response was a swift and brutal 26 percent stock-price decline. If the company's statement signals lower expectations for long-term revenue and earnings, then the steep decline is warranted. On the other hand, if the interruption in growth is truly temporary, a lower stock price represents a buying opportunity.

Examples of important new information include merger and acquisition deals, significant share buyback programs, and meaningful changes in executive incentive compensation. We address the signaling implications for each of these corporate initiatives in chapters 10 through 12.

ESSENTIAL IDEAS

- Before you can consider the likelihood and magnitude of expectations revisions, you need to clearly understand where expectations stand today.

- To read expectations properly, you must think in the market's terms. Expectations investing allows you to tap the benefits of the discounted cash-flow model without requiring you to forecast long-term cash flows.

• You can estimate PIE by using publicly available information sources.

• You should consider revisiting an expectations analysis when stock prices change significantly or when a company discloses important new information.

Appendix: Employee Stock Options and Expectations Investing

In the early 1980s, the biggest component of executive pay was cash. Since then, stock option grants have come to dominate senior executives' pay. Indeed, options are a more significant form of compensation for all employees, especially in high-technology companies. In 2000, the National Center for Employee Ownership estimated that between 7 and 10 million employees were eligible to receive stock options in the United States, a sevenfold increase from the prior decade. We cover the incentive features of ESO programs in more detail in chapter 12. For now, we examine their importance in calculating shareholder value.

Why do companies grant ESOs? The primary reason is that employees create a great deal of a company's future value. As a result, shareholders are willing to share the upside with employees by diluting their own equity. When motivated employees create more value than they cost in dilution, both shareholders and employees win.

Under present accounting rules, companies must disclose the cost of ESOs in footnotes to their financial statements. But the Financial Accounting Standards Board does not require companies to charge the cost against earnings on their income statement.[5] Of course, ESOs do not become more or less costly based on where companies disclose them. Since ESOs can have a meaningful impact on shareholder value, investors must properly recognize them regardless of accounting treatment.

VALUING ESOS

The common practice of ignoring ESOs isn't acceptable, because it can lead to a significant underestimation of costs and liabilities. Past ESO grants are a genuine economic liability—investors should treat them like debt. And future option grants are an indisputable cost of doing business.

Before we present the steps involved in valuing options, let's look at six basic factors that affect option value: current stock price, exercise price, stock-price volatility, time to expiration, risk-free interest rate, and dividend yield.

- *Current stock price.* The payoff to the employee is the positive difference between the stock price and the exercise price on the date that the employee exercises his or her options. Companies almost always establish the exercise price, the price at which an employee can buy the company's stock, at the market price on the date of grant; the exercise price remains fixed over the entire option life, usually ten years. Options are available for exercise after employees become vested, typically three to five years after the grant date.

- *Exercise price.* Options become more valuable as the stock price increases and less valuable as the stock price decreases. But even if the stock price falls below the exercise price, options can retain some value. This value stems from the next two factors—volatility and time to expiration.

- *Stock-price volatility.* Volatility—expressed as standard deviation— is a measure of the uncertainty of future stock-price movements. Higher stock-price volatility increases option value because the stock price is more likely to rise well above the exercise price.

- *Time to expiration.* How long until the option expires also affects ESO value. The longer the time to expiration, the greater the chance that the stock price will increase, and, therefore, the more valuable the option.

- *Risk-free interest rate.* The yield on short-term U.S. treasury securities is a proxy for the risk-free interest rate. If the other five factors stay constant, then the higher the interest rate, the more valuable the option.

- *Dividend yield.* The final factor affecting option value is dividend yield. Since ESO holders do not ordinarily receive dividends, a higher dividend means that the company has less cash to invest to increase the stock price. Hence the higher the dividend, the lower the option value.

Let's consider the six factors together. Assume a ten-year, at-the-money (meaning exercise price equals current stock price) option with 30 percent volatility, about the average for the Fortune 500, and a 2 percent dividend yield. Brian Hall estimates this option to be worth about 40 percent of the stock price.[6] Increase the annual stock price volatility to 70 percent and assume no dividends (conditions more representative of start-ups), and the option value increases to about 80 percent of the stock price. The combination of high volatility and no dividends makes ESOs in start-ups more costly to shareholders than those granted in established, dividend-paying companies.

Valuing Already-Granted Options

How do we integrate ESOs into the expectations investing process? The first part of total ESO value relates to the *options that have already been granted*. The appropriate way to handle already-granted ESOs is to treat them like debt—a deduction from corporate value to arrive at shareholder value. Since most start-ups are equity financed, ESOs—not debt—are their largest liabilities. But unlike debt, the ESO liability rarely appears on the balance sheet. Instead, we must calculate its value using the information tucked away in the financial statement footnotes.

ESOs differ from debt in another significant way. Valuing the liability for outstanding debt is relatively straightforward. It is simply the present value of the fixed contractual cash flows—interest payments and the return of principal. In contrast, ESOs are not a fixed claim but a *contingent* claim. Stock-price performance ultimately dictates the value of ESOs to employees and the cost to shareholders.

We value already-granted ESOs by following three steps.

Step 1: Value the ESOs Already Granted. In most cases, we recommend that you use the option-pricing-model inputs the company provides in the footnotes. Note that as investors, our focus is on the cost of the options to shareholders.[7] Companies generally estimate a time to exercise that is shorter than the option's contractual life to capture the likelihood of early exercise. Doing so lowers the estimated cost of the option grants appropriately.

To illustrate, we value Microsoft's outstanding options at the end of fiscal 2000. Companies typically present their outstanding stock options in groups with similar characteristics. For simplicity's sake, we will value just one of Microsoft's groups. Using the company's assumptions for convenience, we value a group that has 166 million of the 832 million total outstanding options (table 5-2).

TABLE 5-2 Valuation of One of Microsoft's ESO Groups (Fiscal Year 2000)

Range of Exercise Prices	Weighted Average Exercise Prices	Stock Price (30 June 2000)	Time to Expiration	Risk-Free Rate	Volatility (σ)	Dividend Yield	Value of Call Option
$83.29–$119.13	$89.91	$80.00	8.6 years	6.2%	33.0%	0.0%	$41.41

The option-pricing model calculates that each option with these characteristics is worth $41.41.[8] Note that we are using the option's contractual life, not its expected life. If we used an average expected life of six or seven years, which accommodates the likelihood of early exercise, the value of each option is approximately 10 to 20 percent lower.[9] At this point, simply multiplying the per-option value by the number of options may seem reasonable. But we must first make other adjustments.

Step 2: Account for Option Cancellations Owing to Employee Departures. Most companies use ESOs as a tool to retain employees. Consistent with this, option programs generally require employees to exercise or forfeit their options shortly after leaving the firm. Departing employees must return worthless and unvested options to the company.

Microsoft's average option vesting period is about five years.[10] Our goal is to estimate what percentage of the 166-million-share group employees will forfeit. The company provides a detailed schedule of options granted, exercised, and canceled. The data from fiscal 1996 through 2000 suggest a forfeit rate of about 3.6 percent per year (table 5-3).

Assuming a 10-year average option life, the options in our group are about 1.4 years old (10-year life minus the 8.6 remaining life) and have 3.6 years to go before the five-year vesting point. From these numbers, we can determine that employees are likely to forfeit about 12 percent of these options. So rather than counting on 166 million exercised shares, we can assume that the number will be closer to 146 million—

TABLE 5-3   Estimate of Microsoft's Option Forfeit Rate

Year	Number of Options	Annual Cancellations	Option Churn Rate
June 1996	932	28	3.0%
June 1997	954	36	3.8%
June 1998	925	25	2.7%
June 1999	830	30	3.6%
June 2000	799	40	5.0%
		Average	**3.6%**

which reduces the value of the ESO liability to \$6.0 billion (146 ×
\$41.41).[11]

Step 3: Incorporate Tax Considerations. When employees exercise an
option, the difference between the stock price and the exercise price
(i.e., the employee profit) is a tax deduction for the issuing corporation.[12] So in valuing options, we deduct the tax benefit. For example,
stock-option tax benefits reduced Microsoft's fiscal 2000 tax bill by \$5.5
billion. For companies currently losing money, these tax benefits can
become valuable tax-loss carry-forwards as they offset taxes on future
income.

Assuming that Microsoft's tax rate is 35 percent, the tax deduction
for this group is worth 35 percent of the \$6.0 billion liability, or just
under \$2.1 billion. The after-tax liability of the group is the pretax lia-
bility of \$6.0 billion less the tax deduction of \$2.1 billion, or \$3.9 bil-
lion. If we repeat this exercise for all of Microsoft's five ESO groups, we
obtain a total expected after-tax value of about \$30 billion at year-end
fiscal 2000.

Valuing Future Option Grants

The second component of ESOs is the cost of *future grants*. This estimate depends on many factors, including labor market dynamics, the
company's stage of development, and capital market performance. But
the fundamental principle is straightforward: We can view the cost of
options as equivalent to cash compensation. After all, for a given option
grant, there is a level of cash compensation at which employees are
indifferent between the option grant or cash compensation. Options are
no less a cost of doing business than cash compensation. Consequently,
we must incorporate the cost of future option grants into the discounted cash-flow model. In this way, the expectations investing
process captures all future compensation regardless of the form it takes.

We can choose from several ways to estimate the value of future
option grants. One logical way is to look at historical grants, which we
can express as a percentage of sales, on a per-employee basis, or as a percentage of total costs. For example, Microsoft's historical after-tax option
cost averaged about 9 percent of sales over the five years ended fiscal

2000 (table 5-4). However, fiscal 2000 was probably an outlier, as the company gave employees an unusually large grant in an effort to boost morale in the midst of the company's legal imbroglio with the Justice Department. Excluding year 2000, the average annual cost was about 5 percent of sales. We can use this past cost—which properly incorporates option cancellations—as an estimate for future costs of ESO grants.

Naturally, option-based compensation is often very high for start-up companies as they build their executive teams. So simple extrapolations of brief historical results (as the Microsoft data emphasize) can be misleading. The main point is that we must acknowledge future options grants in estimating PIE. Ignoring the cost of ESOs for these companies inevitably leads to an incomplete, and often misleading, view of market expectations.

TABLE 5-4   Microsoft's After-Tax Options Cost as a Percentage of Sales (in millions)

Fiscal Year	Revenue	After-Tax Options Cost	Options Cost as a Percentage of Sales
2000	$22,956	$6,032	26.3%
1999	19,747	882	4.5
1998	17,752	882	5.0
1997	12,959	698	5.4
1996	9,654	547	5.7
		Average	**9.4%**

6
identifying
expectations
opportunities

We now turn to the second step of the expectations investing process, identifying expectations opportunities (figure 6-1). All expectations revisions do not carry the same weight. Some are inevitably more important than others. When you can focus on what matters, you can more efficiently allocate your time to increase your odds of finding high potential payoffs.

The most effective way to accomplish this objective is to isolate the value trigger likely to have the greatest impact on shareholder value. We call this value trigger the *turbo trigger*. The goal is to increase the odds of finding *expectations mismatches*—meaningful differences between the current price-implied expectations (PIE) and future revisions.

FIGURE 6-1   Expectations Investing Process

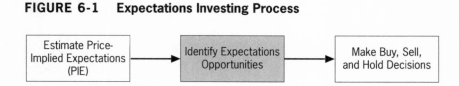

SEARCHING FOR EXPECTATIONS OPPORTUNITIES

Four building blocks—two *data sets* and two *tools*—serve as the foundation for identifying expectations opportunities (figure 6-2). The two data sets are historical performance and PIE. Historical performance serves as a reality check both on the reasonableness of PIE and on your assessment of likely revisions to PIE. PIE encapsulates the market's expectations for a company's future performance.

The two tools are the expectations infrastructure (chapter 3) and competitive strategy analysis (chapter 4). The expectations infrastructure allows for systematic analysis of the underlying sources of shareholder value. Competitive strategy analysis provides perspective on industry attractiveness and a company's chosen strategies. Together these tools yield indispensable insights into potential revisions of market expectations.

FIGURE 6-2   Identifying Expectations Opportunities

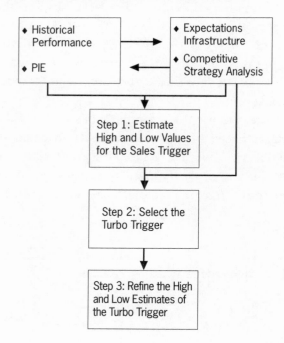

Assessing the Triggers

Three steps are important in the search for expectations opportunities. The ultimate goal of the three steps is to identify the turbo trigger and to refine your estimates of its effect on shareholder value.

Step 1: Estimate High and Low Values for the Sales Trigger, and Calculate the Shareholder Values That Result.

We begin with the sales trigger because sales revisions are likely to produce the most significant changes in shareholder value. Starting with sales allows you to determine quickly whether you should spend time on operating costs and investments, the other two value triggers. The process we recommend reduces your analytical effort substantially because you focus only on what really matters.

To estimate the impact of the sales trigger on shareholder value, you need to do two things. First, estimate high and low scenarios for the sales growth rate. Second, estimate how the sales growth rate affects the operating profit margin via three value factors—price and mix, operating leverage, and economies of scale.

Use the benchmark data (historical performance and PIE) and analytical tools (the expectations infrastructure and competitive strategy analysis) to help shape the high and low estimates for the sales growth rate. For some companies, the three sales-triggered value factors that affect the operating profit margin are not significant enough to warrant detailed analysis. In other cases, value factors are mutually offsetting. For example, market-leading companies such as Wal-Mart and Dell pass on the benefits of economies of scale and cost efficiencies to their consumers through lower prices. Once you determine how the sales trigger affects high and low estimates for the sales growth rate and operating profit margin, calculate the corresponding high and low shareholder values. Study the results. The range depicts the change in stock price from potential sales growth variability. It also defines how great the shareholder value variability must be for the other two triggers—costs and investments—to qualify as the turbo trigger.

Step 2: Select the Turbo Trigger. How do you figure out whether costs or investments qualify as the turbo trigger? Determine how far they must vary from their PIE estimates to have a *greater* impact on shareholder value than the sales trigger.

WHAT ABOUT THE COST OF CAPITAL AND THE MARKET-IMPLIED FORECAST PERIOD?

The search for expectations opportunities should primarily focus on the value triggers and the value driver projections they spawn—not the cost of capital or the market-implied forecast period. Here's why.

Let's start with the cost of capital. Changes in interest rates influence stock prices because they affect discount rates. Often, changes in interest rates, rather than revisions in performance expectations, explain stock-price movements. However, relying on interest rate forecasts for individual stock-selection purposes is a losing game. Shifts in interest rates affect all stocks, albeit to different degrees. If you feel strongly about the direction of interest rates, rebalance your mix of stocks, bonds, and cash.

The forecast periods of companies within the same industry are usually narrowly clustered. If a company's market-implied forecast period is substantially longer or shorter than that of its industry peers, then you should carefully recheck the PIE value drivers to be certain that you have accurately reflected the consensus. Assuming that the company's competitive profile is close to the industry average, a relatively short market-implied forecast period may signal a buying opportunity, and a long period may signal a selling opportunity.

A constant market-implied forecast period is tantamount to continual changes in expectations. For example, assume that a company's forecast period is four years today and that it remains unchanged a year from now. If there truly were no change in expectations, the market-implied forecast period a year from now would be three years rather than four. In this case, an investor who purchased shares priced with four years of value creation expectations receives a "bonus" of an additional year—a positive shift in expectations that brings with it an extra return, assuming that there are no offsetting expectations changes in the company's operating value drivers.

Assume that you estimate the PIE for a stock that currently trades at $20. The high and low estimates of the sales growth rate, filtered through the expectations infrastructure, yield values of $25 and $15, respectively. Using the PIE, calculate how much operating profit margin must vary from the PIE estimate—*owing solely to cost efficiencies*—to create a comparable impact on shareholder value. Look at the result, and consider the likelihood that the margin will be that variable.

Suppose that the PIE operating profit margin is 10 percent and that it would have to range from a high of 17 percent to a low of 3 percent to generate the same shareholder-value impact as the high and low estimates of sales growth rate. If you believe that the margins will almost certainly be between 8 and 12 percent, then the cost trigger is *not* the turbo trigger. You can apply the same procedure to test the changes in the incremental investment rate for the investments trigger.

What if shareholder value *is* sufficiently sensitive to either cost or investment variability so that one of them qualifies as the turbo trigger? In this case, you should revisit that trigger, estimate high and low ranges for the affected value drivers (either operating profit margin or incremental investment rate), and calculate the resulting high and low shareholder values.

Step 3: Refine the High and Low Estimates of the Turbo Trigger, and Calculate the Shareholder Values That Result. Finally, before deciding to buy, sell, or hold, refine your initial estimates of turbo trigger variability. Specifically, drill down one more level to the *leading indicators of value*. Leading indicators are measurable, current accomplishments that significantly affect the turbo trigger and hence shareholder value. Examples include customer retention rates, time to market for new products, number of on-time new-store openings, quality improvements, and average cycle time from order date to shipping date. Two or three key leading indicators typically account for a substantial percentage of the variability in the turbo trigger.

For example, Thomas H. Nodine of L.E.K. Consulting analyzed the leading indicators for The Home Depot.[1] Over 70 percent of The Home Depot's stock price depends on future sales growth. An analysis of sales growth reveals two leading indicators of value—new-store growth and revenue per store. For each 1 percent change in new-store growth, the company's value rises or falls by about 7 percent. Although achieving growth targets is critical, the company must not open new stores so quickly so as to cannibalize sales at existing stores. Meeting new-store targets is so important that a one-year delay in scheduled openings reduces The Home Depot's value by almost 16 percent. Two leading indicators—growth in new stores and revenue per store—largely determine The Home Depot's sales growth rate and expectations revisions for shareholder value.

PITFALLS TO AVOID

We all occasionally fall into psychological traps that keep us from achieving higher investment returns. These traps materialize when we use rules of thumb, or heuristics, to reduce the information demands of decision making. While heuristics simplify analysis, they can also lead to biases that undermine the quality of our decisions. Often, intuition suggests a course of action that more deliberate analysis proves to be suboptimal. Be sure to avoid two common pitfalls—overconfidence and anchoring—when you establish the range of potential expectations revisions. Let's look at these pitfalls more closely.

In the words of Will Rogers, "It's not what we don't know that gets us into trouble, it's what we know that ain't so." Researchers find that people consistently overrate their abilities, knowledge, and skill, especially in areas outside their expertise. For example, when security analysts responded to requests for information that they were unlikely to know (e.g., the total area of Lake Michigan in square miles), they chose ranges wide enough to accommodate the correct answer only 64 percent of the time. Money managers were even less successful, at 50 percent.[2]

Remember the overconfidence trap when you estimate the high and low scenarios for sales growth as part of the initial step in the three-step search for expectations opportunities. Overconfidence in setting the ranges can cause you to misidentify the turbo trigger. An unrealistically broad range overestimates the shareholder-value impact of sales growth variability, leading you to misidentify sales as the turbo trigger. If your estimated range is too narrow, the reverse is true—you may choose one of the other two triggers (costs or investments) when, in fact, you should select sales. When you estimate inappropriate ranges and unrealistically high or low shareholder values, you get misleading buy and sell signals.

How can you avoid overconfidence? There are several simple, practical ways:

- Try not to overestimate your abilities—know thyself.

- Allow for a margin of safety.

- Challenge your high and low estimates.

- Seek feedback from others.

The second pitfall is anchoring, that is, giving disproportionate weight to the first information you receive. As a result, initial impressions, ideas, estimates, or data "anchor" your subsequent thoughts.

Hersh Shefrin cites an apt example: security analysts who revise expectations after corporate earnings announcements. Shefrin suggests that analysts do not revise their earnings estimates enough to reflect new information, because they are anchored on past views. Thus positive earnings surprises lead to more positive surprises, and negative surprises lead to more negative surprises.[3]

One of the most common anchors is a past event or trend. In considering high and low ranges for sales growth, don't give too much weight to historic results at the expense of more salient factors, especially when you analyze companies undergoing rapid change. Stock price is another anchor that creates a major pitfall for investors. Investors often consider a stock cheap if it is at a low point in its trading range and expensive if it is at the high end. So even if the current fundamental prospects of a company justify a change in value, investors often have trouble erasing historical prices from memory.

How do you avoid anchoring? You can take some of the following precautions:

- Realize that past events or prices are signposts, not answers.

- View the decision from various perspectives.

- Seek information from a variety of sources.

GATEWAY CASE STUDY

By continuing our case study of Gateway from chapter 5, we can reinforce much of the analytical terrain just covered. Our goal in chapter 5
was to estimate PIE, so we didn't need to delve into Gateway's strategy
and operations. Now, however, we enlist the tools to draw a more complete picture of the company.

Gateway manufactures, markets, and supports a product line of personal computers (PC). It markets directly to its customers, including
small businesses, individuals, and government agencies. The company
also offers services—such as Internet access, financing, and training—
to fortify its PC business. Gateway had about a 5 percent share of the
global PC market in 2000.

Gateway distributes its PCs in three ways: direct order by phone,
direct order via the Internet, or retail through Gateway Country stores.
This "call, click, or come-in" distribution strategy effectively reaches
Gateway's target market.

Importantly, Gateway has a build-to-order business model, which
means that the company doesn't assemble a PC until it has an order in
hand. In fact, an order generally spends less than one day inside a Gateway assembly facility. Even the retail stores embrace this model: Customers
don't walk out of the store with a computer; rather, they place an order
and receive the custom-assembled computer via a delivery service. In this
way, Gateway can run the business with very modest capital requirements.
Dell, an industry leader, also uses a build-to-order model, but unlike Gateway, it focuses on larger corporate customers rather than individuals and
small businesses. In contrast, competitors like Compaq and Hewlett-
Packard do not use a build-to-order model and therefore need to build
inventory in order to market through distributors and retailers.

The PC industry had sales of over $200 billion in 2000. Historically,
brisk global demand for PCs drove consistent 15 to 20 percent unit-
volume growth.[4] Roughly 40 percent of industry sales are in the United
States.

Competitive Analysis

Thinking about the potential for expectations revisions for Gateway's
stock, we consider three strategic frameworks: five forces, value chain,

and disruptive technology. The five forces and value chain apply because the PC industry is well defined and has easily distinguishable operational activities. The disruptive-technology framework highlights the rapid technological change affecting the industry. Although the PC enjoys a dominant position today, its future is far from assured.

Let's begin with how the five forces may affect expectations:

- *Barriers to entry.* On the surface, barriers to entry do not appear particularly high in this assembly-based business. However, replicating the market leaders' brand strength and operational scale is difficult. Further, Gateway is a leader in the home and small-business markets and has developed specific customer channels to best serve its markets. Threats of new entrants into Gateway's space do not look ominous. These factors point to relatively low variability in its future operating performance.

- *Substitution threat.* For Gateway, the substitution threat comes mainly from new technology: The PC might lose its central position. This threat, though lurking, has yet to materialize at the time of this analysis in April 2000. We discuss this point in greater detail as part of the disruptive-technology framework.

- *Buyer power.* The buyers of Gateway's products—both individual and corporate—are a relatively segmented group, and as such none has significant bargaining power. The PC market, however, is very price competitive, particularly during periods of softening demand. Gateway's trusted brand and low-cost, build-to-order business model make its pricing structure appear to be sustainable. These factors suggest modest variability.

- *Supplier power.* Although Gateway deals with many suppliers, about a dozen account for 80 percent of the company's direct material purchases. Yet supplier power does not appear to be a major threat, because all components are industry standard. Thus, despite more than one-half million potential product configurations, the company can procure materials at a competitive price, maintain lean inventories, and still assure that the necessary components are available as required. Again, variability appears muted.

• *Rivalry among competitors.* Rivalry among competitors in the industry has not been fierce enough to undermine industry profitability. Some of Gateway's competitors—including Compaq and IBM—have heavily discounted their products from time to time to move excess inventory. But these companies deal primarily with large corporations. Gateway escaped these periods relatively unscathed because its target market and business model are sufficiently different from those of the industry titans. Given the competition's significant financial resources, however, potential variability from rivalry is at least moderate and may intensify.

Next we consider variability in the context of *value chain* analysis.[5] We can use the modern value chain as a guide to evaluate Gateway's activities (figure 6-3). Gateway's customers are predominantly individuals and small businesses, and its customer priorities include the following:

• Sales assistance

• Flexible configuration options

• Easy and fast ordering and delivery

• Total hardware, software, and financial solutions

• Life-of-machine technical support

The company uses three *channels* to directly reach customers: telephone (call), Internet (click), and retail stores (come-in). Again, all three channels rely on a build-to-order model. Unlike some of its competitors, therefore, Gateway does not have to forecast demand substantially in advance of sales.

Gateway's *offering* includes PCs and compatible peripherals. The

---

FIGURE 6-3   The Modern Value Chain

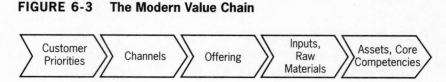

Source: From *The Profit Zone* by Adrian J. Slywotzky and David J. Morrison, copyright © 1997 by Mercer Management Consulting, Inc. Used by permission of Times Books, a division of Random House, Inc.

mix of more than 200 components allows for 600,000 possible configurations. Moreover, the Your:)Ware program aims to solve customers' needs like financing, Internet access, and trade-ins. The company outsources actual delivery of the products to United Parcel Service.

The company's *inputs* include industry-standard components to minimize stock-outs and to assure low direct-material costs.

The company has three *core competencies*: customer contact (before, during, and after the sale), assembly, and supplier network orchestration.

An overarching driver of Gateway's value chain activities is its build-to-order model. It allows Gateway to create shareholder value in three meaningful ways: First, because Gateway has direct customer contact and a firm handle on its inventories, it can guide customers to in-stock parts and components versus those that might be short. Second, by working closely with suppliers, Gateway can assure rapid and reliable component replenishment. Finally, the build-to-order model minimizes physical capital needs, lowering investment requirements and reducing the risk of product obsolescence.

So even though the structure of Gateway's value chain isn't unique—Dell approaches the market similarly—the combination of its value chain activities *and* its target market, individuals and small businesses, is different. This enabled the company to gain substantial market share in the late 1990s.

Finally, we consider the risk of *disruptive technology*. An emerging industry is dedicated to network-computing devices, that is, hardware products that access the Internet, often with wireless technology, and tap the software on network servers as needed. Should network-computing devices take off, they would threaten the PC industry and create significant operating performance variability for PC vendors, including Gateway. Of course, Gateway and its competitors might successfully make the transition. Under any circumstances, the emergence of a disruptive technology would heighten sales variability.

Historical Analysis

An analysis of historical financial results (table 6-1) offers the following clues about future performance variability:

- *Sales growth* decreased substantially over the five-year period, reflecting slower sector revenue growth, offset to some degree by strong market-share gains and nonsystem revenues. At the same time, industry unit-shipment growth decelerated. However, unit-volume growth for the industry and Gateway alike sharply exceeded sales growth because of average unit selling price declines, which reflect cheaper components and competitive pressures. Prospects for continued sector growth, market-share gains, international expansion, and beyond-the-box revenues suggest substantial sales growth potential—as well as execution risk—relative to the 20 percent reflected in the current PIE. In particular, the beyond-the-box initiatives—including software and peripheral sales, Internet access and portal income, financing, warranty, and training—promise substantial growth. Beyond-the-box sales accounted for 9 percent of the company's total in 1999.

- *Operating profit margin* remained in a fairly narrow range, 6.6 to 7.1 percent, excluding the poor 4.6 percent performance in 1997, when the company suffered from an inventory glut. Management responded with lower prices and an inventory write-off, leading to the lower margin. Given the company's sharpened inventory-management skills and beyond-the-box initiatives, another drop in operating profit margin seems unlikely. Gateway's historically stable operating profit margin suggests that the benefits from economies of scale and cost efficiencies are passed on to consumers in the form

TABLE 6-1   Gateway's Historical Operating Value Drivers

	1995	1996	1997	1998	1999	Five-Year Average
Sales growth rate	36.1%	37.0%	25.0%	18.7%	15.8%	26.2%
Operating profit margin	6.8%	7.1%	4.6%	6.6%	6.9%	6.4%
Incremental fixed-capital investment rate	9.8%	4.1%	18.7%	11.1%	17.4%	12.2%
Incremental working-capital investment rate	14.3%	−10.3%	−5.5%	−35.6%	8.3%	−6.6%

Source: Gateway, Inc.

Note: Five-year averages are geometric.

of lower selling prices. Since Gateway's preproduction costs are relatively low, operating leverage is not a critical value factor.

• *Investments.* In the mid-1990s, the business consumed a modest amount of working capital as it grew. However, by 1999, Gateway managed to achieve a negative cash conversion cycle (table 6-2). The cash conversion cycle is the sum of days in inventory and days in receivables, less days in payable. When a company receives cash for the goods it sells *before* it pays its suppliers, the cycle is negative. So as it expands, working capital becomes a source of cash. Given the company's tight working-capital management, we anticipate little future variability.

Since Gateway does not manufacture components—such as microprocessors, disk drives, and graphics cards—it does not have to invest in significant fixed capital. It has only to set up assembly lines, which require relatively low investment. Although the rollout of retail stores has increased its capital requirements, Gateway's total investment needs have been, and are likely to remain, relatively modest.

Both competitive and historical analyses point to sales growth as the most likely turbo trigger. But before we draw this conclusion, let's go to the numbers.

Table 6-3 presents Gateway's PIE, introduced in chapter 5. The numbers reflect an April 2000 stock price of $52 and consensus forecasts from Value Line and analyst reports. The preceding competitive analysis and historical overview provide the background for the three steps for identifying expectations opportunities.

We first follow step 1, estimating the high and low values for the sales trigger and calculating the shareholder values.

Our analysis and discussions with leading analysts point to a sales

---

TABLE 6-2   Gateway's Cash Conversion Cycle (1995–1999)

	1995	1996	1997	1998	1999
Days sales outstanding	32	31	27	26	25
Days in inventory	20	22	18	13	10
Less: Days payable outstanding	24	29	31	37	43
Cash conversion cycle	28	24	14	2	(8)

Source: Gateway, Inc.

growth range of 6 to 28 percent over the seven-year forecast period. Here's the rationale:

- *Low.* The bottom of the range, 6 percent, assumes a slowdown in worldwide PC unit growth to a mid-single-digit rate. It also assumes that Gateway will continue to gain only modest market share, and that the company's beyond-the-box initiatives will not continue their strong growth.

- *High.* The 28 percent growth rate at the high end of the range builds in strong gains in beyond-the-box sales and anticipates solid market-share gains in a vibrant consumer/small-business PC market. The high-end number is also consistent with management's stated objective, outlined in February 2000, of reaching $30 billion in sales in 2004.[6]

We established the sales growth range taking into account the first two value factors—volume, and price and mix. The sales trigger also affects operating profit margin via operating leverage and economies of scale, as well as price and mix.

Let's begin with price and mix. Gateway's emphasis on higher-margin, beyond-the-box services accounts for the improvement in operating profit margins from historical levels to those anticipated in PIE. Specifically, beyond-the-box sales are expected to reach over 40 percent of the corporate total by 2006. Gateway's stated long-term goal is to maintain overall operating profit margins by offsetting the higher margins from its beyond-the-box initiative with lower selling prices for its PC hardware business. In other words, lower PC prices will counterbalance future benefits from mix improvement.

The 6 percent low-end sales growth scenario would have a mate-

TABLE 6-3   Gateway's Price-Implied Expectations—Value Drivers

Sales growth rate	20.0%
Operating profit margin	9.0%
Cash tax rate	35.0%
Incremental fixed-capital rate	11.0%
Incremental working-capital rate	−5.0%

rial negative impact on operating profit margins. Slower industry growth is likely to result in intense price competition; causing selling price declines to be greater than cost declines. In addition, the price competition would spill over to the beyond-the-box initiative, shrinking operating profit margins due to the negative affect of price and mix.

Operating leverage and economies of scale do not appear to be material factors in Gateway's margins. Operating leverage tends to be important for companies that have large preproduction costs and uneven investment spending patterns. Neither categorization fits Gateway. Further, although Gateway may enjoy economies of scale as it grows, most industry observers believe that competition will assure that the company passes most of those benefits to consumers in the form of lower prices.

The combination of the company's business model, competitive circumstances, and management strategy suggests limited variability in operating profit margin for the consensus and high-end scenarios. We assume that Gateway's improved sales mix in 2000 will increase its operating profit margin to 9 percent, and the margin will remain stable thereafter. We assume 6 percent operating profit margins for the low-end sales growth scenario, reflecting the deleterious effect of price and mix.

We are now ready to determine the impact of the range of sales growth rates on shareholder value. Here are the numbers:

| | GROWTH RATE | | | ESTIMATED VALUE | | CHANGE IN VALUE | |
	PIE	Low	High	Low	High	Low	High
Sales	20%	6%	28%	$18.05	$76.35	−65%	47%

These data tell us that if we were to revise expectations for Gateway's sales growth rate from 20 percent to 6 percent, the stock would retreat by 65 percent, from $52 to $18.05 per share. Alternatively, an upward shift in anticipated sales growth from 20 percent to 28 percent would spark a 47 percent rise to $76.35 per share.

The next step in identifying changes in expectations is to select the turbo trigger.

What would it take for the costs and investments triggers to change value more than sales does? Cost efficiencies, or inefficiencies, would have to add or subtract about 3 percentage points, or 300 basis points, to the PIE operating profit margin of 9 percent in order to be as material as sales growth. Given Gateway's cost structure, that magnitude of expectations revision seems highly unlikely. *So we conclude that operating costs will not be as important as sales.*

The incremental fixed-capital rate would need to *quadruple*, or become significantly *negative*, for it to generate the same per-share variability that sales generates. Expectations for the incremental working-capital rate, too, would need to undergo extreme revisions to have an

WHAT'S IN A TARGET PRICE?

We are establishing a . . . price target of $96 for Gateway shares . . . based on a 40X multiple to our FY01 [fiscal year 2001] EPS of $2.41.[a]
—Wall Street analyst

Wall Street analysts love to provide target prices as much as investors love to see them materialize. Most analysts, however, concoct target prices by slapping assumed multiples on estimates of accounting-based earnings. As a result, they provide little if any substance in understanding expectations.

Can the expectations investing process shed any light on target prices? Absolutely. Here's how to decipher them.

Start by understanding the PIE for the current stock price, and then determine the turbo trigger. Now you're ready to go.

Using the target stock price, determine how well the turbo trigger will have to perform. In Gateway's case, sales growth rate expectations would have to increase from the 20 percent consensus level in PIE to 33 percent to justify the target price, all else being equal. Analysts would surely be surprised by what their price targets imply about the future financial performance of the companies they cover. And until they move from the world of accounting to PIE, they won't know what's in a target price.

[a]Richard Gardner, *Salomon Smith Barney Equity Research*, 14 April 2000.

impact comparable to that of sales. Again, the business model, competitive landscape, and historical results all suggest that such results are highly unlikely. *We can confidently conclude that investment is a less significant trigger than sales.* The analysis confirms that sales is Gateway's turbo trigger.

Much of the analytical heavy lifting is now complete. But we still need to refine our estimate of changes in shareholder value triggered by sales. What are the leading indicators for Gateway's sales growth? First, we need to assess the contributors to sales growth embedded in PIE. Table 6-4 shows a breakdown of Gateway's base year sales and the anticipated growth rate for the three major segments.

Three leading indicators appear critical. The first is the overall growth of the consumer PC market. The consumer market was about 50 percent of Gateway's business in 1999. Consumer PC unit-volume growth for the industry is expected to stay at about 14 percent until about 2006.[7] However, analysts anticipate that dollar sales growth will rise at roughly one-half the unit-volume growth rate because of an expected 7 percent annual decline in average selling prices.

Analysts expect Gateway's unit volume to grow faster than the industry's, suggesting ongoing market-share gains from its relatively modest global base. If consumer PC unit-volume growth for the industry comes in at a faster-than-expected 17 percent and Gateway captures its anticipated market share, the company's unit-volume growth will be 24 percent. Net of lower selling prices, Gateway's consumer PC sales growth would be above-consensus 17 percent, triggering an approximate $3 increase in the value of Gateway shares. A reduction in expec-

---

TABLE 6-4   Gateway's PIE for Sales Growth by Business Segments (in millions)

Segment		SALES		Compounded Annual Growth Rate
		1999	2006	
Consumer	48%	$4,150	$10,383	14%
Small business	37%	3,200	7,075	12%
Beyond the box/other	15%	1,295	13,251	40%
Total	100%	$8,645	$30,979	20%

tations for industry unit-volume growth rate to 6 percent represents about $8 per share of downside (table 6-5).

The second leading indicator is growth in the small-business market. Gateway's launch of Country stores supports penetration of both the small-business and consumer markets. Country stores combine the physical retail-shopping experience—the touch and feel of the actual products—with the direct model, as each purchase still goes through the build-to-order system. Thus, Country stores offer the benefits of a store without the cost of inventory, which is significant, given the high rate of product obsolescence in the PC industry. These stores also offer customer training.

Analysts expect the small-business market to advance at a 10 percent unit-volume rate, with Gateway growing at a rate not quite double that of the market. Declining selling prices for hardware mean that sales will grow at a slower rate than that of unit volume. Should unit volume in this market grow at a rate closer to 14 percent, with Gateway gaining its expected market share, the company's stock price would increase by approximately $2 (table 6-6). On the other hand, a 2 percent small-business volume growth rate, with the same market-share assumptions, would reduce stock price by $7.

The final leading indicator is the most important one: Gateway's beyond-the-box revenue growth—which includes financing options, peripheral products, and training. In the fall of 1999, Gateway announced a wide-ranging relationship with America Online (AOL). As part of the pact, AOL became the de facto Internet service provider for Gateway customers, with its service marketed alongside Gateway.net on all Gateway computers. Gateway and AOL share the profits from the

TABLE 6-5   Gateway's Consumer PC Sales Growth Scenarios

	Growth	Stock Impact	Issues
High	17%	+$3	• Spread of Internet user base • Rapid increase in e-commerce • Increase in broadband connections
PIE	14%		
Low	5%	−$8	• Emergence of information appliances • Developing market for used PCs • Saturation in established markets

subscriptions. AOL also serves as the fulfillment center for Gateway.net, performing billing, network, and content functions. In addition, the deal includes the development of a co-branded, online software store and the joint marketing of information appliances.[8]

If beyond-the-box revenue growth comes in at 55 percent (the high end of its range), then Gateway's value per share increases by $19 (table 6-7). A 14 percent growth rate, in contrast, translates into a $19 stock-price decline.

Management's ambitious 2004 sales goal implies a 28 percent compounded annual growth rate for the company. To meet this objective, not only must beyond-the-box sales climb at a 55 percent rate, but both the consumer and small-business sectors must come in at the high end of expectations as well. The April 2000 price of $52 plus the sum of the stock-price changes implied by the high-end scenarios ($3 for consumer PC, $2 for small-business PC, and $19 for beyond-the-box) equals $76.

In early 2001, about a year after our analysis, Gateway stock was trading in the low twenties. Why? The stock fell sharply when Gateway announced sharply lower-than-expected sales and earnings for the fourth quarter of 2000. Its bleak announcement signaled a longer-term slowdown in consumer PC spending because of faster-than-expected market saturation, rapidly increasing competition from information appliances, and growing concerns about the economy.

In chapter 5 and this chapter, we discussed the first two steps of the expectations investing process: estimating PIE and identifying expectations opportunities. We are now ready to take the final step, which takes what we've learned from the first two steps and translates it into buy

---

TABLE 6-6   Gateway's Small-Business Sales Growth Scenarios

	Growth	Stock Impact	Issues
High	16%	+$2	• Downsizing and productivity focus • Rapid increase in e-commerce • Rapid new business formation
PIE	12%		
Low	3%	−$7	• Emergence of information appliances • Developing market for used PCs • Saturation in established markets

TABLE 6-7   Gateway's Beyond-the-Box Sales Growth Scenarios

	Growth	Stock Impact	Issues
High	55%	+$19	• Higher rate of PC purchasers buy services • Technological change accelerates training needs • Strong strategic partners
PIE	40%		
Low	14%	−$19	• Emergence of information appliances • Competition in services market • Commoditization of PC services

and sell decisions. It completes the journey—from PIE to buy (or sell)—and is the subject of the next chapter.

ESSENTIAL IDEAS

• If you know which expectations revisions are most important, then you improve your odds of finding high potential payoffs.

• Four building blocks constitute the foundation for identifying expectations opportunities. Historical results and PIE give us the data, and competitive strategy analysis and the expectations infrastructure give us the analytical tools.

• Identifying expectations opportunities embodies three steps:

• Step 1: Estimate high and low values for the sales trigger, and calculate the shareholder values that result.

• Step 2: Select the turbo trigger.

• Step 3: Refine the high and low estimates of the turbo trigger, and calculate the shareholder values that result.

• Beware of behavioral traps as you estimate ranges.

7

buy, sell, or hold?

We now turn to the third and final step in the expectations investing process: the buy, sell, or hold decision (figure 7-1). In this chapter, we show how to translate expectations opportunities into investment decisions. We do this by converting anticipated expectations revisions into an expected value for a stock. We then compare expected value with the current stock price in order to find *expectations mismatches*—buying or selling opportunities. Finally, we provide specific guidelines for when to buy, sell, or hold stocks.

EXPECTED-VALUE ANALYSIS

You have identified the turbo trigger and formulated expectations that differ from the consensus. But that is not enough to make a confident

FIGURE 7-1   Expectations Investing Process

buy or sell decision. No analysis is complete without accounting for risk. You must acknowledge that the future direction of market expectations is highly uncertain. Fortunately, you can structure this uncertainty to gain a better idea of the relative attractiveness of a stock with *expected-value analysis.*

Expected-value analysis is extraordinarily useful for evaluating uncertain outcomes. Expected value is the weighted average value for a distribution of possible outcomes. You calculate it by multiplying the *payoff* for a given outcome, in *- case stock price or shareholder value, by the *probability* that the outcome materializes. You then sum up the results to obtain expected value. Think of it as a single number that captures the value of a set of possible outcomes.

So how do you determine the payoffs and the probabilities? You do it by estimating the payoffs, using the process presented in chapter 6. Essentially, you isolate the turbo trigger, analyze its impact on operating value drivers for a range of plausible outcomes, and calculate the resulting shareholder value for each outcome.

Estimating sensible probabilities for high, low, and consensus (i.e., price-implied expectations) scenarios is a challenge. Investors often rely on certain rules of thumb that, though useful, also promote biases. Here are three biases to avoid when you establish probabilities.[1]

- Avoid relying on recent memory to assess the likelihood of a future outcome. The danger is that you will assume that recent or vivid events are more likely to recur than they really are. For example, say that a company reports quarterly earnings below consensus expectations because of onetime or transitory factors. If you then mistakenly increase the probability of the low-end turbo trigger forecast, you risk missing an investment opportunity.

- Avoid judging the likelihood of an outcome by linking it to similar, but unrelated, outcomes. For instance, don't assume that an event that affects one company necessarily affects its competitors similarly.

- Avoid starting with an untested assumption and assigning probabilities to outcomes based on that assumption. Misleading historical precedent may influence your initial assumption. Consider the case of historical growth rates. Investors often assume that past growth rates will continue, notwithstanding significant changes in the competitive environment.

Expected-value analysis highlights two essential ideas:

- If value variability is *high* (that is, if the range of payoffs is wide), then a stock can be attractive or unattractive *even if the consensus outcome is the scenario with the highest probability.*

- If value variability is *low*, then *you must bet against the consensus* to achieve superior returns.

Let's begin with high variability. Assume that the value range for a $42 stock is $10 at the low end and $90 at the high end. Let's say that you attach a 50 percent probability to the consensus value, and 15 percent and 35 percent probabilities to the low and high values, respectively. This combination of payoffs and probabilities yields an expected value of $54 per share, as table 7-1 shows. The expected value is nearly 30 percent greater than the $42 current stock price. So even if the consensus has the highest probability of being right, a sufficiently wide range of value variability can signal an attractive buy or sell opportunity. In this case, the relatively high upside value of $90 per share coupled with a relatively robust 35 percent probability triggers the buy opportunity.

Now let's examine low variability, which represents relatively predictable companies with well-specified business models. We apply the same probabilities as before, but the high value is now $55 instead of $90, and the low value is $35 instead of $10. In this case, we see that the 8 percent difference between the expected value of $45.50 and the $42 current price is not large enough to be conclusive (table 7-2). The margin of safety is too small.

TABLE 7-1   Expected Value with High-Variability Scenarios

Stock Price	Probability	Weighted Value
$10	15%	$ 1.50
42 (current)	50%	21.00
90	35%	31.50
Expected value		$54.00

TABLE 7-2   **Expected Value with Low-Variability Scenarios (Consensus Is Most Likely)**

Stock Price	Probability	Weighted Value
$35	15%	$ 5.25
42 (current)	50%	21.00
55	35%	19.25
Expected value		$45.50

TABLE 7-3   **Expected Value with Low-Variability Scenarios (Non-consensus)**

Stock Price	Probability	Weighted Value
$35	10%	$ 3.50
42 (current)	20%	8.40
55	70%	38.50
Expected value		$50.40

Using the same value range as that in table 7-2, let's look at non-consensus probabilities, where the consensus is *not* the most likely scenario. Table 7-3 shows a high-end scenario with a 70 percent probability, a low-end scenario with a 10 percent probability, and a consensus scenario with just a 20 percent probability. The expected value of $50.40 is well above the prevailing price because of the high probability attached to the high-value scenario. So it is easy to see that non-consensus probabilities can trigger a buy or sell decision even for a company with low-value variability. In this situation your decision to buy or sell is a bet *against* the consensus estimate.

GATEWAY CASE STUDY

Let's apply this kind of analysis to the Gateway case. In chapter 5 we estimated Gateway's PIE based on a $52 stock price. The analysis in chapter 6 pointed to sales as the turbo trigger with the following shareholder-value payoffs from the range of sales-growth-rate estimates:

	GROWTH RATE			ESTIMATED VALUE		CHANGE IN VALUE	
	PIE	Low	High	Low	High	Low	High
Sales	20%	6%	28%	$18.05	$76.35	–65%	47%

We now examine three possibilities: (1) that the most likely scenario will be the consensus; (2) that it will be non-consensus and bearish; and (3) that it will be non-consensus and bullish.

- *The consensus.* We assume a 50 percent probability that the consensus sales growth will materialize, a 20 percent probability for the low value, and 30 percent for the high value. The expected value of $52.52 is close to the $52 current stock price (table 7-4). So attaching a high probability to the consensus does not induce an obvious buy or sell decision.

- *Non-consensus and bearish.* For this scenario, we assume an 80 percent chance that the low-end value materializes, and 15 percent and 5 percent probabilities for the consensus and high-end ranges, respectively. With these revisions, the expected value decreases to $26.06 per share, or 50 percent below the $52 stock price (table 7-5). The stock is therefore a clear candidate for sale.

- *Non-consensus and bullish.* Finally, let's consider a case in which you estimate a high probability that expectations will shift toward the high end of the sales growth range. Specifically, an 80 percent probability for the high value, 15 percent for the consensus, and only 5 percent for the low value lead to an expected value of $69.78 per share (table 7-6). In this case, the stock is a buy candidate.

The Gateway case underscores the key message: For companies with low value variability, a non-consensus point of view is essential for a buy or sell decision. As value variability increases, however, you can get clear buy or sell signals even when the consensus view is the most likely.

A stock's expected value is rarely static. As payoffs and probabilities change, so too will expected values. To avoid overlooking profitable

---

TABLE 7-4 Gateway's Expected-Value Calculation (Consensus)

Sales Growth	Stock Value	Probability	Weighted Value
6%	$18.05	20%	$ 3.61
20%	52.00	50%	26.00
28%	76.35	30%	22.91
		100%	$52.52

TABLE 7-5   Gateway's Expected-Value Calculation
             (Non-consensus and Bearish)

Sales Growth	Stock Value	Probability	Weighted Value
6%	$18.05	80%	$14.44
20%	52.00	15%	7.80
28%	76.35	5%	3.82
		100%	$26.06

TABLE 7-6   Gateway's Expected-Value Calculation
             (Non-consensus and Bullish)

Sales Growth	Stock Value	Probability	Weighted Value
6%	$18.05	5%	$ 0.90
20%	52.00	15%	7.80
28%	76.35	80%	61.08
		100%	$69.78

expectations mismatches, you should update expected value calculations whenever important new information becomes available or whenever there is a meaningful change in stock price.

Once you establish the difference between expected value and the stock price, you are ready to consider whether to buy, sell, or hold. Specifically, look at the following three questions:

• When should I buy a stock?

• When should I sell a stock?

• How do time and taxes affect the decision?

THE BUY DECISION

Let's begin with the buy decision. Stated simply, whenever you estimate that the expected value is greater than the stock price, you have a potential opportunity to earn an excess return.[2] However, the prospect of an excess return is by itself not enough to signal a genuine buying opportunity. You still must decide whether the excess return is sufficient to warrant purchase.

Your decision depends on two factors. The first is the stock price's percentage discount to expected value, or its margin of safety. The greater the discount to expected value, the higher the prospective excess return—and the more attractive a stock is for purchase. Inversely, the higher a stock's price premium to its expected value, the more compelling the selling opportunity.

The second factor is how long it will take for the market to revise its expectations. The sooner the stock price converges toward the higher expected value, the greater the excess return. The longer it takes, the lower the excess return. By the same logic, when expected value is below the current stock price, the faster the price converges toward expected value, and the greater the urgency to sell the stock.

Table 7-7 shows the excess returns for various combinations of price/expected values and number of years for expectations to converge. Let's say you figure a stock is trading at 80 percent of its expected value. Further assume that the market will take two years to adjust its expectations to yours. You can expect to earn an annual 13 percent excess return above the cost of capital.[3] If expectations stay the same thereafter, the stock will generate no additional excess returns.

Remember that buying opportunities do not depend on the absolute level of company performance or investor expectations, but rather on *your expectations* relative to *price-implied expectations*. A high-expectations stock is still attractive if the company delivers results that spur investors to revise their expectations upward. Likewise, a low-expectations stock is no bargain if you believe that the company's prospects warrant those expectations.

Before we leave the buy decision, we urge that you avoid falling into the escalation trap. Investors tend to make choices that justify past decisions. Past investments of money or time that cannot be recovered create what economists call *sunk costs*. Even though investors know that

---

TABLE 7-7   Excess Returns on Stock Purchase below Expected Value

		NUMBER OF YEARS BEFORE MARKET ADJUSTS				
		1	2	3	4	5
	60%	73.3%	32.0%	20.4%	15.0%	11.8%
Price/	80%	27.5%	**13.0%**	8.5%	6.3%	5.0%
Expected Value	100%	0.0%	0.0%	0.0%	0.0%	0.0%

Assumes a 10 percent cost of equity capital.

sunk costs are irrelevant to current decisions, some find it hard to divorce the two.

Investors manifest this behavior when they escalate their commitment to a stock by buying even more of it after it has declined. Not only are investors slow to take losses, but they often buy *more* of a stock just because they bought it in the past. Of course, prior investment decisions are history, and decisions today need to be based on today's expectations, not yesterday's. As Warren Buffett says, "The most important thing to do when you find yourself in a hole is to stop digging." Investors who stick to the recommendation of buying stocks only when they trade at a sufficient discount to their expected value will avoid the irrational escalation trap.

How a problem or set of circumstances is presented can also affect people's decisions. Even the same problem framed in different—and objectively equal—ways can cause people to make different choices. One example is what Richard Thaler calls *mental accounting*.[4] Say that an investor buys a stock at $50 per share and it surges to $100. Many investors divide the value of the stock into two distinct parts: the initial investment and the profit. And many treat each part differently—the original investment with caution and the profit portion with considerably less discipline.

This "house-money effect" is not limited to individuals. Hersh Shefrin documents how the committee in charge of Santa Clara University's endowment portfolio succumbed to this effect. Because of strong market performance, the endowment crossed a preordained absolute level ahead of the time line that the university president set. The result? The university took some of the "house money" and added riskier investment classes to its portfolio, including venture capital, hedge funds, and private placements.[5]

THE SELL DECISION

You might choose to sell for three potential reasons:

1. *The stock has reached its expected value, and your updated, expected-value estimate is lower than the stock price.* A note of caution is in order here. Investing is a dynamic process. Expectations are a mov-

ing target that you must periodically revisit and revise. Investors who mechanistically sell shares just because they reach an out-of-date target price potentially sacrifice significant returns. Selling because a stock has reached its expected value only makes sense if your most recent analysis leads you to expect no further upside.

2. *Better opportunities exist.* Investors who actively manage their portfolios will ideally choose to hold the stocks that are most attractive today. Consequently, they embark on a never-ending search for the stocks that trade at the largest discounts relative to their expected value.

   The availability of more attractive stocks than those currently in the portfolio gives rise to the second reason to sell. This decision rule is different from the first one because you do not have to presume that stocks reach their expected values to sell.

   Basically, as long as you maintain your targeted level of diversification, you should consider selling a stock in your portfolio with a higher price/expected-value ratio and use the proceeds to buy a stock with a lower price/expected-value ratio. In the next section, we will show how taxes affect your decision to sell.

3. *You have revised your expectations downward.* Sometimes, even thoughtful and detailed analysis misses the mark. At other times, unanticipated events prompt you to change your expectations—and sometimes materially. If a downward revision in your expectations results in an unattractive price/expected-value relationship, the stock becomes a sell candidate.

You also need to avoid certain pitfalls when selling stocks. For example, people are very averse to losses when making choices between risky outcomes, no matter how small the stakes. Daniel Kahneman and Amos Tversky find that a loss has about *two and a half times* the impact of the gain the same size.[6] In other words, people feel a lot worse about losses of a given size than they feel good about a gain of similar magnitude.

Because investors don't want to take a loss, they tend to sell their winners too soon and hold on to their losers too long. All investors, including those who adopt the expectations investing approach, should try hard to sidestep this trap.

Terrance Odean confirms the loss-aversion phenomenon in a study of 10,000 accounts at a large discount-brokerage firm.[7] He finds that investors indeed realize their gains more readily than their losses. And the winning investments that investors chose to sell continue to outperform the losers they hold on to in subsequent months. The moral is that we risk making poor decisions when we rely on purchase price as the frame of reference.

Another pitfall to avoid is the confirmation trap. Investors often seek out information that supports their existing point of view while avoiding information that contradicts their opinion. This trap not only affects where investors go for information, but also influences how they interpret the information they receive. After purchasing a stock, investors often fall into the confirmation trap by seeking evidence that confirms their thesis and dismissing or discounting information that refutes it.

We have found one technique particularly useful for managing the confirmation trap in the expectations investing process: Ask questions, and conduct an analysis that challenges your most cherished and firmly held beliefs about the company and industry. Posing disconfirming questions opens your mind to alternatives that you haven't fully considered. An open mind improves your decision making and, ultimately, your investment track record.

THE ROLE OF TAXES

As we've just seen, investors sell a stock for three reasons: It has reached its expected value, better opportunities exist, or you revise your expectations downward. But before you sell a stock for any of these reasons, you must consider the role of taxes. Replacing a fairly valued stock with a stock priced below its expected value may turn out to be a bad idea after you take the tax consequences into account.[8]

Let's say that you found a stock trading below its expected value and bought it for $100. One year later, the stock is trading at its expected value of $125, yielding you a handsome 15 percent excess return over the 10 percent market return for equity. Should you sell the stock?

It depends. Consider two possibilities. The first is that you hold the stock for another year and earn a cost of equity return of 10 percent. This scenario, of course, assumes that expectations don't change during that year. By the end of the year, the stock has risen by 10 percent, from $125 to $137.50.

Now consider a second possibility. Suppose you sell the stock instead and reinvest the proceeds into another stock. What return would you have to earn on the second stock in the next year to justify the move? It turns out you'd have to earn about a 15 percent return—a 5 percent excess return—to make the move worth your while. That's because you would have to pay a 20 percent long-term capital gains tax rate on the $25 gain, or $5. After taxes, only $120 is available to invest in the next stock. An investment of $120 would have to earn a return of nearly 15 percent to generate the same $137.50 end-of-year value as holding the current stock. The required return would have to be even higher if we were to incorporate transaction costs into the analysis. After properly accounting for taxes and transactions costs, you sometimes do better holding a fairly valued stock than selling it and buying a new stock trading only modestly below its expected value.

Overconfidence also plays a role in excessive stock trading, which is very tax inefficient and incurs high transaction costs. Brad Barber and Terrance Odean studied account data for over 60,000 households from a large discount-brokerage firm. They found that the 20 percent of investors who traded most actively earned an average net annual return 5.5 percent lower than that of the least active traders.[9] Overconfident investors make more mistakes because they trade more often and rack up unnecessary costs along the way.

ESSENTIAL IDEAS

- Whenever the expected value is greater than the stock price, you have an opportunity to earn an excess return.

- The magnitude of the excess return depends on *how much* of a discount a stock trades relative to its expected value and *how long* the market takes to revise its expectations. The greater the stock price discount and the sooner the market revises its expectations, the greater the return.

• As an investor, you have three potential reasons to sell: A stock reaches its expected value, a more attractive stock exists, or your expectations have changed.

• Before you decide to sell a stock, consider the important role of taxes and transactions costs.

• Beware of behavioral traps before you buy or sell.

8

beyond discounted
cash flow

As you step through the expectations investing process, you will run across companies with price-implied expectations that are vastly more optimistic than what industry norms lead you to expect, as well as what existing businesses can ever deliver. In these cases, *automatically* concluding that expectations are too optimistic would be a mistake. For companies fraught with uncertainty, stock price is the sum of discounted cash-flow value (representing the existing businesses) plus *real-options value*. Real options capture the value of uncertain growth opportunities. In this chapter, we show you how to use some straightforward real-options valuation techniques to increase the power of expectations investing.[1] We also introduce the notion of reflexivity, that is, how stock prices can affect business fundamentals.

To be sure, the discounted cash-flow model is all you need to estimate the expectations for most businesses. But many investors have come to question the model's role in valuation since the model does not easily explain why some money-losing start-ups enjoy such large market capitalizations. We argue that the discounted cash-flow model is as relevant as ever—as long as you complement it with a real-options analysis for certain companies.

Real-options analysis is critical for two types of companies in particular—start-ups and reinventors. Start-ups are companies with limited operating track records; most are companies that have gone public in recent years. Most start-ups, for example, still need to invest significant sums to build infrastructure, establish brand identity, and acquire customers. Few of these companies have meaningful revenue streams. Fewer yet are profitable.

Reinventors operate in fast-changing sectors and continually "start up" new businesses within their existing organization. Enron is a good example. During the 1990s, Enron transformed itself from a domestic natural-gas pipeline company into a global trader of gas, electricity, water, and telecom bandwidth. Along the way, it started many new and uncertain businesses.

REAL OPTIONS

The real-options approach applies financial options theory to real investments, such as manufacturing plants, product line extensions, and research and development.[2] A financial option gives its owner the right, but not the obligation, to buy or sell a security at a given price. Analogously, companies that make strategic investments have the right, but not the obligation, to exploit these opportunities in the future.

Real options take a number of forms, including the following:

- If an initial investment works out well, then management can exercise the option to *expand* its commitment to the strategy. For example, a company that enters a new geographic market may build a distribution center that it can expand easily if market demand materializes.

- An initial investment can serve as a platform to *extend* a company's scope into related market opportunities. For example, Amazon.com's substantial investment to develop its customer base, brand name, and information infrastructure for its core book business created a portfolio of real options to extend its operations into a variety of new businesses.

- Management may begin with a relatively small trial investment and create an option to *abandon* the project if results are unsatisfactory. Research and development spending is a good example. A company's future investment in product development often depends on specific performance targets achieved in the lab. The option to abandon research projects is valuable because the company can make investments in stages rather than all up-front.

Each of these options—expand, extend, and abandon—owes its value to the flexibility it gives the company.

As many investors and managers know, a project with zero net present value—the present value of the future cash flows equals the current outlay to achieve those cash flows—may still have significant value. Flexibility is often the additional source of value.

Flexibility adds value in two ways. First, management can defer an investment. Because of the time value of money, managers are better off paying the investment cost later rather than sooner. Second, the value of the project can change before the option expires. If the value goes up, we're better off. If the value goes down, we're no worse off because we don't have to invest in the project.

Traditional valuation tools, including discounted cash flow, can't value the contingent nature of the exploitation decision: "*If* things go well, *then* we'll add some capital."[3]

The Strategic-Investment-Option Analogy

We can draw a strong analogy between the real options to expand and extend a business and a financial call option.[4] This option analogy works well when a company has the opportunity to grow beyond its usual line of business. You should include "business as usual" growth in the discounted cash-flow analysis, and use the real-options method to consider the value of large and/or more innovative projects that differ from the norm.

While the analogy from a real option to a financial call option is not perfect, it is informative. The insights you'll get from real-options analysis include an understanding of when a company might exercise an option, what triggers the exercise decision, and what role uncertainty plays in the value of a growth option.

Figure 8-1 lists the inputs you need to value real options and their financial call option counterparts. Although the Black-Scholes equation is the best-known tool for valuing financial options, all the option valuation methods use the following five variables:[5]

1. *Value of project, S:* the present value of the project's expected free cash flow.

2. *Cost to exercise the option, X:* the onetime incremental investment required to exercise the option at time *T*. (Note that *X* is in future dollars, and *S* is in current dollars.)

3. *Project volatility, σ:* a measure of the potential variability of the project's future value.

4. *Life of option, T:* how long a company can defer an investment decision without losing an opportunity; usually measured in years.

FIGURE 8-1   Mapping an Investment Opportunity onto a Call Option

Investment Opportunity	Variable	Call Option
Value of Project	S	Current Stock Price
Cost to Exercise the Option	X	Exercise Price
Project Volatility	σ	Stock-Price Volatility
Life of Option	T	Life of Option
Risk-Free Rate of Return	r	Risk-Free Rate of Return

Source: Reprinted by permission of *Harvard Business Review.* From "Investment Opportunities as Real Options" by Timothy A. Luehrman, July–August 1998, 52. Copyright © 1998 by the Harvard Business School Publishing Corporation; all rights reserved.

5. *Risk-free rate of return, r:* the interest rate on short-term government debt. We need not estimate a risk-adjusted discount rate (cost of
capital) to value an option, because σ fully accounts for project risk.

For example, a company might expand its distribution system in
two years if volume continues to grow. The company estimates that it
will have to spend $40 million at that time to build a new distribution
center ($X = \$40$ million), and based on today's best forecast, the present
value of the incremental free cash flow is $30 million ($S = \$30$ million).

If the current forecast proves true, this project would have a negative
net present value when management makes it decision in two years, as
the expected benefits (S) are less than the costs (X). This negative value
holds even if we compare the present value of cost to present value of
benefits. (For example, using a risk-free discount rate of 5 percent, the
present value of the cost is $36.3 million, which is still greater than the
expected benefits.) But since volume *could* surge, the option to expand
is valuable even when it looks like the company may not use it. Discounted cash flow is the correct valuation tool when X is not discretionary, or when spending X is not contingent on some future outcome.
When management has the flexibility to defer or reject an investment,
however, discounted cash flow undervalues the project since it assumes
that management will pursue even value-destroying projects.

In this example, management will make a decision at the end of two
years, when it will reestimate S. If at that time S is greater than X, then
the company will decide to expand because the project has a positive
net present value. If at the time of the decision S is less than X, then the
project will have a negative net present value and the company won't
expand. Today, two years before the decision, we need to value the flexibility to defer or reject the investment—that is, we need to value the
real option.

Let's continue with our example of the distribution expansion to
show how to use the five inputs in an option calculation. Thus far we
have established that S equals $30 million, X equals $40 million, and T
equals two years. Assume that volatility is 50 percent per year and the
risk-free rate is 5 percent per year. When we plug these inputs into an
options calculator such as the Black-Scholes formula, we find that the
option to expand the distribution system is worth $6.4 million.

We don't need to understand the intricacies of an option-pricing model to understand what fundamentally increases real-options value. Value rises when the net present value $(S - X)$ increases, when we extend the time we have to defer decisions (T), or when volatility (σ) heightens.

Valuing Real Options

We can always directly calculate the value of a real option using the Black-Scholes formula. But a lookup table that covers the likely range of inputs is much more intuitive. Table 8-1 is an adaptation of such a table, from Richard Brealey and Stewart Myers.[6]

The table reduces the five option inputs to a simple two-by-two lookup table. Panel A shows the value of a two-year growth option, and panel B shows the value of a three-year growth option, both as a percentage of S. We filled the cells of the table by repeated calculations using the Black-Scholes formula.[7] We present a range of volatility that encompasses low- and high-volatility industries.

Across the columns, we consider various S/X ratios. Note that the

TABLE 8-1   Option Value Lookup Table

Panel A: Time to Expiration = 2 years

		S/X				
		0.50	**0.75**	**1.00**	**1.25**	**1.50**
	0.25	0.9%	7.3%	18.6%	30.5%	40.6%
Annual	0.50	10.3	21.2	31.3	39.9	47.1
Volatility	0.75	23.9	34.9	43.4	50.1	55.4
(σ)	1.00	37.8	47.5	54.4	59.6	63.7
	1.25	50.7	58.7	64.2	68.2	71.3

Panel B: Time to Expiration = 3 years

		S/X				
		0.50	**0.75**	**1.00**	**1.25**	**1.50**
	0.25	2.8%	11.9%	23.8%	35.0%	44.1%
Annual	0.50	17.4	29.0	38.6	46.2	52.4
Volatility	0.75	34.6	44.8	52.3	57.9	62.3
(σ)	1.00	50.5	58.7	64.2	68.3	71.4
	1.25	64.0	70.1	74.1	77.0	79.2

Option values expressed as percentage of S; $r = 5\%$; European option.

cost to exercise, X, is at the time of decision. To calculate a company's cost *today*, we take the present value of X, that is, $X/(1+r)^T$. Consequently, real options are more "in the money" when you consider X on a present-value basis. (It adds two to five percentage points to the option value as a percentage of S.) Of course, a prerequisite to legitimate real-options value is that a company has either financing on hand to exercise its options or else access to capital at the time of exercise.

When S/X equals one, the net present value of the project at the time of decision is zero.[8] When S/X is greater than one, the net present value for the project at the time of decision is positive; when it's less than one, the project's net present value is negative.

Two key factors drive potential project value, S/X. The first is the rate of return on investment that is likely given the company's competitive position and the overall returns in the industry. The higher the assumed rate of return, the higher the S/X ratio. We also must consider competitors' option exercise strategies.[9] Competition in many industries drives returns down to a cost-of-capital level (an S/X of 1.0). The second factor is the level of past real-options-enabling investments. Companies that have made substantial options-enabling investments can pursue new opportunities with a lower incremental investment than can a company that hasn't.[10]

The other big driver of option value is volatility, the range of variability on the future value of S. In the rows in table 8-1, we show a range of values for σ. A call option, for example, has downside protection built in. The higher the potential value of S, the more valuable the option. However, increasingly lower potential values of S do not decrease option value, because once S is sufficiently low, a company will not exercise the option. Thus, higher volatility leads to higher option value.

Volatility is an intrinsic characteristic of a project's future value, but it is often difficult to measure precisely. For stock options, the corresponding input is the volatility of the future stock returns, which investors either estimate from historical stock return data or infer from traded stock options.[11]

Some large business projects simply expand or extend the current business model, so we can reasonably use stock-price volatility as an estimate of the range of potential project values. Other projects lead to new business models that differ markedly from the company's current model.[12] One word of advice: Be sure that your estimate of volatility corresponds to the new business's range in value.

To demonstrate how to use the lookup table, let's recalculate the option to expand the distribution centers. The original inputs are as follows:

S = $30 million

X = $40 million

σ = 50 percent

T = 2 years

r = 5 percent per year

In this case, the S/X ratio is 0.75. Panel A in table 8-1 gives us an option value that is 21.2 percent of S, or $6.4 million.

The lookup table provides several immediate insights about real options:

• Real-option value increases as S increases relative to X (scan from left to right on the table), as volatility increases (scan from top to the bottom), and as option life extends (compare panel A with panel B).

• Real options are valuable even when S is far below X. (Look at the option values under S/X = 0.50 and S/X = 0.75.) Discounted cash flow ignores this value and undervalues assets with embedded options.

• Real-option value is bounded. Note that none of the option values in the table exceeds the value of the underlying asset, S.

Even though table 8-1 is small and compact, it covers a large range of volatility and potential project values. As a rough point of calibration, consider the following volatility benchmarks:

• The average company has annual stock-price volatility in the range of 40 to 50 percent.

• Pharmaceutical companies have rather low volatility of about 25 percent per year.

- High-tech stocks often have annual volatility of 75 to 90 percent per year.

- Biotechnology and Internet companies have volatility as high as 90 to 125 percent per year.[13]

We constructed table 8-1 for only two- and three-year options because a company can defer investments for only a short time in competitive product markets. Options with long lives are often follow-on options—available only if a company successfully executes the first near-term option. The value of these follow-on options is generally only a small fraction of the near-term real-options value.

WHEN TO USE REAL-OPTIONS ANALYSIS IN EXPECTATIONS INVESTING

Most of the literature on real options addresses corporate managers and their asset-allocation decisions. Our concern here is when expectations embedded in the stock price are above the industry norm, and when part of those expectations potentially represent real options. The goal is to use this thinking to decide whether to buy, sell, or hold individual stocks.

The first step is to evaluate companies and their stocks across two dimensions. The first dimension is *potential real-options value*, a judgment of whether the company is likely to have significant real-options value. The second dimension is *imputed real-options value*, or the value that the market is already placing on any real options that might be present.

Under what conditions are potential real-options values significant?

- First, there must be a high level of *uncertainty*, or volatility of outcomes. Industries with low volatility have scant real-options value. For example, consulting firms are low-volatility businesses. Because they essentially sell labor by the hour, they find it difficult to generate huge upside surprises.

- The *management* team must have the strategic vision to create, identify, evaluate, and nimbly exploit opportunities in a dynamic environment. The existence of real options doesn't guarantee that a company will capture their value. Speed and flexibility are especially important for translating real-options potential into actuality. Real-options success is especially elusive for larger companies that have many layers of management, which slow the decision-making process.

• The business must exhibit *market leadership*. Market-leading businesses tend to get the best look at potentially value-creating opportunities to expand or extend their business. Companies like Cisco and Intel, for example, have "proprietary" growth options not available to their competitors by virtue of their market-leading positions. Market leaders can also reinforce the proprietary nature of their real options, preserving more of their value for themselves.

Let's turn now to *market-imputed real-options value*. This is the difference between the current stock price and the consensus-driven discounted cash-flow value for the existing businesses.

Measuring market-imputed real-options value is a straightforward extension of the expectations investing approach. Basically, you estimate price-implied expectations for the existing businesses (chapter 5) with one significant alteration: Instead of *solving* for the market-implied forecast period, you *assume* a forecast period for the existing businesses.

Here's why. Solving for the forecast period improperly uses stock price (which may include real-options value) to "read" expectations that reflect only the *existing businesses*. Therefore, the market-implied forecast period will always overstate the "correct" period for an options-laden company—and sometimes by a significant number of years.[14]

The difference between the market value of equity and the estimated value of existing businesses is potentially real-options value (figure 8-2).

Your challenge is to determine whether the expectations behind the market-imputed real-options value are reasonable.

Some ambiguity between the existing business value and real-option value doesn't undermine the expectations investing process. In fact it highlights its strength, because expectations investing tests the reasonableness of the *sum* of the existing business value and imputed real-options value. Since this sum always equals the current market price, any over- or undervaluation of the existing business value reduces or increases imputed real-options value by the same amount.

We've developed a simple matrix that helps you understand when you need a real-options analysis in the expectations investing process (figure 8-3). You can use the matrix to determine when the potential for real-options value doesn't match the real-options value embedded in the stock price. The matrix has four quadrants:

- *No real-options analysis required (low-potential/low-imputed real-options value).* This combination, in fact, fits most established companies. In this case, all you need is the standard expectations investing process (chapters 5 through 7).

- *Buy candidate (high-potential/low-imputed real-options value).* In essence, you are placing a higher value on real options than the market is. Provided the difference is large enough, the stock is a buy candidate.

- *Sell candidate (low-potential/high-imputed real-options value).* Here the reverse case is true—that is, the market is valuing real options more highly than you are. Provided that the difference is sufficiently large, the stock is a sell candidate.

- *Real-options analysis required (high-potential/high-imputed real-options value).* This quadrant is where more detailed real-options analysis promises the greatest potential rewards for investors. The

---

FIGURE 8-2 Imputed Real-Options Value

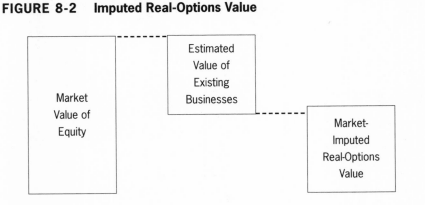

rest of this section focuses on companies that fall into this quadrant.

Your ultimate goal is to assess the reasonableness of the project value and the total investment outlay needed to justify the imputed real-options value. In other words, can the company live up to the potential implied by the stock price? To answer that question, you will have to determine whether the implied scale of the company's opportunity and investments is consistent with market size, access to capital, management resources, and competition.

THE VALUE OF REAL OPTIONS IN AMAZON.COM

Amazon.com offers an instructive case on the value of real options. In February 2000, Amazon was the canonical example of a company with large potential and imputed real-options value. At the time of our analysis, it traded at about $64 per share, a market capitalization of nearly $22 billion. But what combination of existing business value and real-options value justified the price?

FIGURE 8-3   Potential versus Imputed Values for Real Options

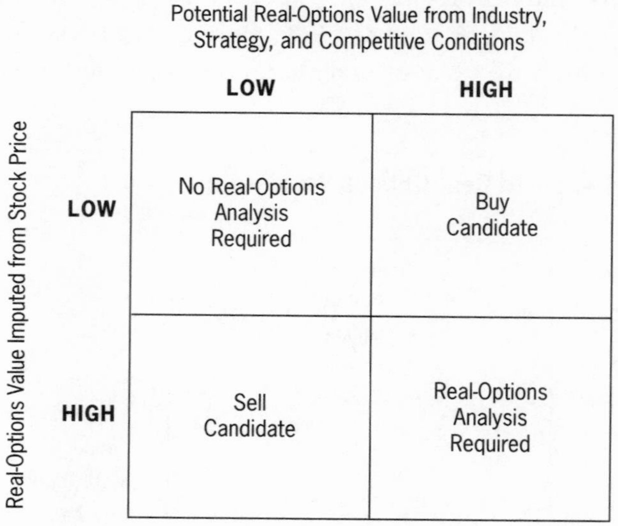

Potential Real-Options Value from Industry,
Strategy, and Competitive Conditions

	LOW	HIGH
LOW	No Real-Options Analysis Required	Buy Candidate
HIGH	Sell Candidate	Real-Options Analysis Required

Real-Options Value Imputed from Stock Price

The expectations investing process analyzes real-options value in four steps:

Step 1: Estimate the Potential Real-Options Value. Amazon fits the bill of a company with significant *potential* real-options value for the following reasons:

- It competes in the highly uncertain business-to-consumer e-commerce market. Rapid category growth, competitive threats, expansion opportunities, and evolving business models all contribute to this uncertainty.

- The management team, led by founder and CEO, Jeff Bezos, had proven adroit in creating, identifying, and exercising real options in the past. Examples included successful forays into the music and video business.

- Amazon was a clear market leader—a company with potential economies of scale and economies of scope. This leadership also allowed it to partner advantageously with other industry heavy-weights, including Microsoft and America Online.

Step 2: Estimate the Imputed Real-Options Value from the Stock Price. Using historical information, Value Line Investment Survey forecasts, Wall Street analyst research reports, and our own assessment of Amazon's prospects for its existing businesses, we established five-year forecasts for sales growth, operating profit margin, and incremental investment. We then extended these forecasts by another five years to cover an assumed ten-year forecast period. Sales growth was the uncontested choice as the turbo value trigger.

Amazon's forecasted annual sales growth for its existing businesses was about 48 percent for the first five years and 40 percent for the second five years. For Amazon to achieve this clip, it would have to achieve significant market share in its various businesses. Further, the discounted cash-flow model assumed that it could reach pretax operating profit margins of almost 8 percent.

With these expectations Amazon's existing businesses were worth

$35 per share, net of employee stock options. In other words, investors could attribute $29 of the company's $64 stock price to imputed real-options value (table 8-2). The $29 per share figure translated into about $10 billion in value.[15]

Step 3: Derive the Requisite Size of the Project Value (S) and the Investment Expenditure (X). We assumed that the appropriate S/X ratio for Amazon was 0.75—which means that Amazon's cost to exercise its strategic options was greater than the present value of its incremental free cash flows. Since we assumed that the real options would expand Amazon's current business, we used the stock's historic volatility of about 100 percent. Finally, we assumed a two-year time to maturity. Using table 8-1 (panel A), we see that the real-options value is about 48 percent of S.

We can use these data to ask two interesting questions: How large does the potential project value (S) have to be to justify an imputed $10 billion real-options value? How large is the potential real-options exercise cost (X) that justifies a $10 billion real-options value?

We establish S as follows: The imputed real-options value is $10 billion. The potential real-options value is 48 percent of S. If imputed equals potential, then S must be just under $21 billion—which suggests a $21 billion market opportunity.

We establish X as follows: The imputed real-options value is $10 billion. For the potential real-options value to equal the imputed value, X must be equal to $28 billion if S is $21 billion and the S/X ratio is 0.75. In other words, investors are pricing Amazon's stock as if they believe that the company can invest $28 billion during the next two years to execute its real option.

TABLE 8-2   Amazon.com's Imputed Real-Options Value

Stock price (22 February 2000)		$64
Existing business value	53	
− Employee stock option liability	−18	
Net existing business value		35
Imputed real-options value		$29 × 345 million shares = $10 billion

To do a sensitivity analysis on these results, we can let S/X vary. (Note that we don't alter volatility, which is an intrinsic feature of Amazon.) For example, if we use an S/X of 1.0, both S and X equal about $18 billion.

Step 4: Assess the Reasonableness of the Numerical Results for S and X. Let's start by considering the reasonableness of the market opportunity (S). In essence, Amazon must have a $21 billion market opportunity today to justify a $10 billion imputed option value (given an annual volatility of 100 percent). Is the magnitude of this market opportunity reasonable?

Let's now assess the reasonableness of X. The $28 billion investment is substantial. Using a liberal interpretation, Amazon's investments for the prior three years totaled under $2 billion.

The reasonableness of S and X raised some key questions:

- What additional e-commerce markets could Amazon profitably pursue?

- Could Amazon overcome the cultural and institutional barriers to successfully expand into international markets?

- What additional fee-based products could the company add?

- How could it leverage its customer database?

- Can any company really spend this much and receive the same returns as it can on a smaller investment? Or does the scale lead to diminishing returns?

With the benefit of hindsight, it appears that the imputed real-options value was indeed too high. Amazon's stock price languished in 2000, falling to $15 per share in early 2001. The stock's descent was the result of lowered expectations for its established businesses and was sufficiently steep to extinguish most of the $29-per-share real-options premium.[16] The shrinkage of this premium turns out to be a self-fulfilling prophecy.

Since start-ups like Amazon depend almost entirely on equity to finance their growth, a depressed stock price makes it practically impossible for the company to finance the very investments that legitimate its real-options value. In other words, the lower stock price effectively withdrew the financing that Amazon needed to execute its options, and thus created doubt about the viability of its growth options. As a result, Amazon's real options became virtually worthless. This analysis underscores the vital feedback loop between stock price and business fundamentals.

REFLEXIVITY

Investors and corporate managers widely accept that the stock price reflects expectations for a company's future financial performance. However, investors devote scant attention to the idea that the *stock price itself can affect that performance.* An important feedback mechanism materializes when stock prices affect business fundamentals, which is important to consider in expectations investing—particularly for young, high-technology companies, which depend heavily on a healthy stock price.[17]

George Soros calls this dynamic feedback loop *reflexivity.* He sums it up this way: "Stock prices are not merely passive reflections; they are active ingredients in the process in which both stock prices and the fortunes of companies whose stocks are traded are determined."[18] We now consider the impact of reflexivity for start-ups in two critical activities—the ability to finance growth and the ability to attract and retain key employees.

Financing Growth

Young companies typically depend on equity financing. Those that consistently report below-expectations performance cast doubts about the viability of their business models. The resulting depressed stock price makes issuing new shares either unduly expensive or simply not feasible. This situation, in turn, impedes or eliminates the implementation of the company's value-creating growth strategies. As investors come to recognize the problem, the stock price often continues its downward spiral.

This spiral not only restricts the company's ability to grow; in some cases it leads to bankruptcy or a takeover at a sharply discounted price.

One such victim was Living.com, a home-furnishings company, which filed for Chapter 7 bankruptcy in August 2000. According to the company's CEO, Shaun Holliday, "the recent downturn in the capital markets has substantially impaired our ability to raise the capital required to achieve profitability."

Many start-ups rely on acquisitions to build their businesses. And most of them fund the deals with stock, which is just another way to finance the company's growth.[19] Poor stock-price performance makes acquisitions for stock either prohibitively costly or simply impossible. Even companies with robust stock prices should not be beguiled into thinking that issuing stock is without risk. If the market gives a thumbs-down to one acquisition by decreasing the acquirer's stock price, it will almost certainly be more circumspect about future acquisitions.

Attracting and Retaining Key Employees

Start-ups often compete in exceptionally tight labor markets and are extremely vulnerable if they cannot offer credible prospects of large stock-option gains to their current and prospective employees. A depressed stock price quickly shrinks options value, threatening a company's current performance and future prospects. Again, as investors recognize the situation, the spiral of decline is likely to continue.

A weak stock price also undermines the confidence of other key constituents, including customers, suppliers, and potential strategic partners. This situation only serves to compound a company's woes.

Ramifications of Reflexivity

What are the implications of reflexivity for expectations investors? First and foremost, investors need to ask whether they have considered reflexivity in their assessment of expectations for the company. Uncritical acceptance of a company's growth strategy, without factoring in the financing risk arising from poor stock performance, is a recipe for disappointing investment results.

We suggest that, at minimum, you evaluate this outcome as the worst-case scenario when you develop a stock's expected value. The probability of this outcome depends significantly on management's vision and execution skills—as well as on top management's ability to convince the market that the company has a sound business model that deserves a high stock price, despite continuing operating losses. In the final analysis, investors in rapidly growing, capital-constrained start-ups must recognize that these young companies bear not only the normal operating risks of any company but also the risk that a stock-price decline will keep the company from executing its growth strategy.

ESSENTIAL IDEAS

- The discounted cash-flow model can understate the value of flexibility, which can lead to a misreading of price-implied expectations for uncertainty-laden start-ups and reinventors.

- Real options capture the potential value of uncertain future opportunities.

- To determine whether you need real-options analysis, consider both a company's potential real-options value and its market-imputed real-options value.

- You should incorporate the dynamic feedback loop from fundamentals to stock and *from stock price to fundamentals*—reflexivity—into the expectations investing process.

9

across the
economic
landscape

Tectonic shifts in stock market value—especially owing to the gyrations of technology stocks—have prompted some investors to suggest that we need new rules to understand value. We emphatically disagree. Fundamental economic principles endure, and they are sufficiently robust to capture the dynamics of value creation across all types of companies and business models. The principles of value creation—which are central to the expectations investing process—are the ties that bind all companies.

Why, then, all the talk about new rules and new paradigms? Principally, investors find that traditional yardsticks, like price-earnings multiples, no longer explain what's happening in the market. They then go on to use proxy measures (e.g., market value per subscriber, market value per page view) that they believe better represent how the market values various industries. In reality, it's not that the market values companies in myriad ways—the market's fundamental valuation model is consistent—it's that the characteristics and properties of businesses vary.

To demonstrate this point, we classify businesses into three broad categories—physical, service, and knowledge—and highlight the distinguishing characteristics of each. We then analyze the value factors that help us identify the most likely sources of meaningful expectations revisions for each of the three categories. What emerges is that the flexible structure of expectations investing allows us to implement it across the economic landscape.

BUSINESS CATEGORIES

We start with a definition of the three business categories. Although we know that the activities of many companies fall into more than one category, our goal in classification is to help define the factors that shape cash flow and expectations revisions.

- *Physical.* For physical companies, tangible assets such as manufacturing and sales facilities, equipment, warehouses, and inventory are critical to creating value. Prominent examples include industries such as steel, auto, paper, and chemicals as well as consumer-oriented sectors, including retailers, restaurants, and lodging.

- *Service.* Service companies rely on people as the main source of advantage and generally deliver their service on a one-to-one basis. Banks, advertising firms, consulting firms, and financial-services companies fall into this category. Sales increases depend on employee growth and productivity. Not surprisingly, employee costs are typically a sizable percentage of total costs.

- *Knowledge.* People are the main source of competitive advantage for knowledge businesses as well. But rather than tailoring services for individual customers, these businesses use intellectual capital to develop an initial product, and then reproduce it over and over again. Software, music, and pharmaceutical companies are prominent examples. Innovation and shifting tastes assure that knowledge businesses must constantly improve existing products and create new ones.

Category Characteristics

Fundamental economic tenets apply to all businesses. But the various categories have different characteristics and hence different paths to expectation revisions.

Investment Trigger and Scalability. Physical businesses must add physical assets, and service businesses must add people, to support their growth. In other words, the need for additional *capacity* triggers reinvestment. This periodic need for capacity limits *scalability*, or the ability to sustain sales growth at a faster rate than the growth of costs. In contrast, scalability is high for knowledge companies because their goods, once developed, are relatively cheap to replicate and distribute.

Netscape founder, Marc Andreessen, considered the scalability distinction between service and knowledge businesses when he positioned his subsequent venture, Loudcloud. Loudcloud's plan was to get into the Web hosting business, a well-populated competitive space. But Andreessen explained that he wanted a new angle: "The dumb way to do this business would be to try to do what other companies do. . . . For every customer, we could hire another 10 people to get them up and run them. It would work. But at the end of the day, there wouldn't be that much value. The business would only scale by the number of bodies you could hire. We wanted to do this for hundreds and then thousands of customers without having to hire that many new bodies."[1] For this reason, Loudcloud designed a scalable business model based on software, not on people.

So why aren't all knowledge companies highly scalable? One reason is that the market accepts relatively few knowledge products. And those that the market does accept often become obsolete quickly. The perpetual threat of product *obsolescence,* in turn, triggers a new round of investment.

Bill Gates, Microsoft's chairman and chief software architect, highlighted the obsolescence risk in a 1998 *Fortune* interview: "I think the multiples of technology stocks should be quite a bit lower than the multiples of stocks like Coke and Gillette, because we are subject to complete changes in the rules. I know very well that in the next ten years, if Microsoft is still a leader, we will have had to weather at least three crises."[2]

Rival versus Nonrival Goods and Protection. Physical and service businesses often enjoy a reduction in their average unit costs as sales increase, up to a point. Beyond that, unit costs again rise as the company bids for additional, scarce inputs or gets bogged down in size- or bureaucracy-induced inefficiencies. This is a world of decreasing returns.

In contrast, some knowledge companies are free from the limitations that scarce inputs impose, because the nature of the goods they produce is different. The distinction is between rival and nonrival goods.[3] With a rival good, an individual's consumption or use reduces the quantity available to others. A car, a pen, and a shirt are examples. In contrast, knowledge companies produce nonrival goods, which many people can use at once. The company creates an initial version of the good, often at great cost, which it can then replicate and distribute relatively inexpensively. Software is the prototype. Since the additional use of these goods does not rely on scarce inputs, greater output and low incremental costs lead to increasing returns.

The ability to protect usage is another distinction between rival and nonrival goods. Strong property rights assure that the owners of physical assets benefit from them. But since knowledge goods are easy to transmit, the risk of unauthorized use is high, which means that the developers of knowledge assets run a greater risk of not receiving compensation for their investment. This issue was the crux of the uproar over Napster, the leading digital file-sharing company, in 2000. Napster facilitated the free exchange of music files between individuals. Music fans could download their favorite tunes while the content creators (the artists and music labels) went unpaid. The result was a legal rift.

Supply-Side versus Demand-Side Economies of Scale. Supply-side economies of scale arise in physical and service companies when they perform key activities at a lower per-unit cost as volume increases. Importantly, supply-side-driven economies of scale generally run into limits well before companies can dominate their markets, because organizational and bureaucratic inefficiencies set in. Accordingly, companies in physical or service categories rarely command dominant market shares.[4]

Economies of scale for knowledge companies hinge on positive feedback, which makes the strong get stronger and the weak get weaker. It is the *demand* side, however, not the supply side, that drives these economies of scale. People want to use a ubiquitous product because it assures compatibility with other users. Microsoft's PC operating system,

America Online's instant messaging, and eBay's auction services are instructive examples. And because the cost of an incremental unit tends to be very low for a knowledge business, positive feedback often intensifies as new members join the user community. This effect leads to winner-take-most outcomes.

Figure 9-1 summarizes the characteristics of these business categories. Within categories and industries, however, companies often embrace vastly different business models, or blueprints for how a company seeks to create shareholder value. The blueprints include strategic choices in areas like product quality, technology, cost position, service, pricing, brand identification, partnerships, and distribution channels. These choices and the category characteristics shape the behavior of sales, costs, and investments in the expectations infrastructure.

A final category difference, although a noneconomic one, is the accounting for investments. Physical companies invest primarily in tangible assets, which they record as assets on the balance sheet and expense (through depreciation) over the estimated useful lives of the assets. In contrast, service and knowledge companies invest primarily in people. The entire amount of these investments is expensed in the year that the company makes the outlay.[5]

Whether companies invest mainly in knowledge versus physical assets does affect earnings and other accounting ratios. But how accountants choose to record an investment *does not* affect the value of the company. For purposes of estimating value, a $1 million investment in

FIGURE 9-1   Primary Characteristics of Various Business Categories

	Physical	Service	Knowledge
Source of advantage	Assets	People	People
Investment trigger	Capacity	Capacity	Product obsolescence
Scalability	Low	Low	High
Products	Rival	Mixed	Nonrival
Protecting capital	Easy	Hard	Hard
Economies of scale	Supply-side	Supply-side	Demand-side

expensed knowledge is the same as a $1 million investment in deprecia-ble tangible assets. What we know in each case is that a company spent $1 million and that the company's value ultimately depends on the cash flows that the investment generates.

BUSINESS CATEGORIES AND THE VALUE FACTORS

We now look at the categories through the lens of the value factors. (For simplicity's sake, we combine our first two value factors: volume, and price and mix). Our goal is to show that the expectations infrastructure (figure 9-2) is sufficiently robust to capture the dynamics of all the cat-egories and thereby help us identify potential sources of expectations revisions.

FIGURE 9-2   The Expectations Infrastructure

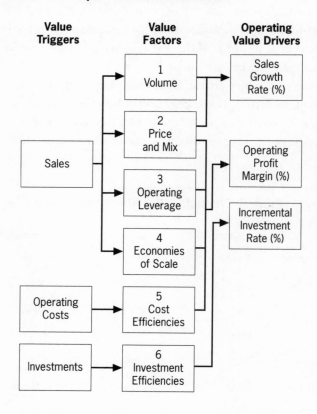

Volume, and Price and Mix

For a physical business, sales growth links to tangible-asset growth and utilization. Think of a retail store chain. Opening more stores or reconfiguring existing stores can raise sales growth expectations. Sales growth and physical assets move together somewhat linearly. Some retailers do better than others because of superior business models or execution skills. But ultimately, sales growth relies on asset growth.

The story for service businesses is similar. Head-count growth and employee productivity drive sales increases. For example, a brokerage firm grows by adding new professionals and getting more production out of its in-place professionals. The level of sales and the number of employees are closely related. *Growth and productivity in assets and people spur sales growth revisions for physical and service businesses, respectively.*

Knowledge businesses are somewhat different. Specifically, two conditions can lead to extraordinary, and often unanticipated, sales growth for knowledge companies. The first is when a product becomes a de facto standard, like Microsoft Windows in PC operating systems. Having one standard assures compatibility among users and allows companies writing complementary applications software to focus their resources on that standard. Often, companies battle to become a standard, but once one company pulls ahead, positive feedback leads to eventual market dominance.

Second, demand tends to take off when a company forms a network that reaches critical mass, that is, the point at which enough people use a product or service to catalyze self-sustaining growth.[6] This growth is the direct result of network effects, which exist when the value of the product or service grows as new members use it.[7] To illustrate, online auctioneer eBay needed a large enough group of buyers and sellers to get to critical mass. But once it reached that point, eBay became the network of choice. Buyers and sellers now go to eBay *because* others are there, and not only are new members valuable to future adopters, but they also benefit those already in the eBay family.

The pattern of adoption and sales growth for standard-setters and network stewards is similar. Growth starts slowly at first, but then it *increases at an increasing* pace. This demand-side-driven growth is a prime area of expectations revisions for the winners, who gain the lion's share of the market, and for losers, who see their potential customers flock to their rival.[8]

Lest we appear overly enthusiastic about the economics of knowledge companies, let us sound a warning. For every winner in a winner-take-most market, we see many losers. Like the winners, these losers shoulder large investment costs. But unlike the winners, they do not generate sufficient revenue to offset the costs. The challenge, of course, is to separate the winners from the losers.

Sales growth is a function of volume as well as price and mix. Some physical and service companies can drive sales growth and higher operating profit margins by raising selling prices, improving their product mix, or doing both. Businesses that offer consumers greater perceived value than their competitors do can sometimes charge premium prices. Doing so affords them the opportunity to grow sales faster than costs. Further, some companies enhance their margins by improving their product mix. However, we know of no companies that have created long-term shareholder value solely by raising prices or improving mix. Nevertheless, these value factors can be a short-term source of expectations revisions.

Operating Leverage

All businesses incur *preproduction costs*, that is, costs incurred before their products or services generate sales. The significance of preproduction costs, as well as the time between the initial cost outlays and sales, varies across categories and companies. Preproduction costs are invariably sunk, however, and companies leverage them only as sales materialize.

Some physical businesses must commit large amounts of capital in advance of sales to have sufficient capacity to meet expected demand. The near-term result is unused capacity. As a company increases sales and uses its capacity, it realizes operating leverage as it spreads its preproduction costs over more units. The result is a reduced average unit cost and higher operating profit margins.

Steel processing is a good example. A new steel facility costs anywhere from $400 million for a mini-mill to $6 billion for an integrated mill.[9] And since it is not feasible to build only part of a steel mill, companies must invest the entire amount before any sales can materialize. Not surprisingly, capacity utilization, a rough index of operating leverage, is one of the key performance measures for the industry. The steel industry is noted for having excess capacity—which is one reason for its dismal performance. Kirby Adams, president of BHP Steel, puts it succinctly: "We must start focusing on building value and not building capacity."[10]

Most knowledge products have high up-front preproduction costs but relatively modest costs of replication and distribution.[11] Software is a classic example. As we noted in chapter 4, Microsoft spent about $2 billion developing Windows 2000. But once it created the first disk, the company could reproduce it at a very low cost. Because the cost of the product is largely fixed, an increase in units sold lowers the per-unit cost.

Drug development is another knowledge business with high preproduction costs.[12] The U.S. Office of Technology Assessment says it can cost anywhere from $200 to $350 million and take from 7 to 12 years to move a product through development and final approval by the Food and Drug Administration.[13] But operating leverage is significant as unit demand grows. One estimate shows the average cost of a new pill declining from $350 million for the first pill to 36 cents for the billionth.[14]

Operating leverage does not indefinitely expand operating profit margin. Rather, we should view it as a transitory phenomenon because physical and service businesses need to add capacity when they run out, and knowledge businesses must develop a new generation of products to avoid obsolescence. But operating leverage can still be an important source of an expectations revision.

Economies of Scale

As a company grows—whether it be physical, service, or knowledge—it often can generate economies of scale that reduce its per-unit costs. Companies that successfully capture economies of scale enjoy higher operating profit margins.

One straightforward example of scale economies is volume purchasing. Larger companies often pay less for their inputs—from raw materials and supplies to intangibles like marketing and advertising services—when they purchase in bulk from their suppliers.

The Home Depot, the world's largest home improvement retailer, demonstrates the power of scale. The company's gross margins widened from 27.7 percent in fiscal 1995 to 29.9 percent in fiscal 2000 as it tacked on more than $30 billion in incremental sales. The company attributed the margin expansion primarily to a lower cost of merchandising, resulting from product-line reviews and increased sales of imported products.[15] In other words, The Home Depot uses its size to get the best possible prices from its suppliers. According to industry analysts, the company passes some of the benefit to consumers in the form of lower prices, and it preserves some of the gain in the form of higher margins. Notably, smaller competitors do not enjoy the same benefits. The home-improvement industry's number two player, Lowe's, had gross margins 1.7 percentage points lower than The Home Depot's in fiscal 2000.

Economies of scale reflect a company's ability to perform activities at a lower cost as it operates on a larger scale. In contrast, the *learning curve* refers to the ability to reduce unit costs as a function of cumulative experience. Researchers have studied the learning curve for thousands of products. The data show that for the median firm, a doubling of *cumulative* output reduces unit costs by about 20 percent.[16] Benefits from the learning curve, therefore, generate higher operating profit margins.

A company can enjoy significant economies of scale without benefiting from the learning curve, and vice versa. But frequently the two go hand in hand. If you understand the distinction between the two, you can better understand past performance and anticipate expectations shifts. For example, if a large company lowers its costs as a result of scale economies, average unit costs will increase if sales subsequently decrease. In contrast, if the company lowers its costs as the result of learning, unit costs may not increase as sales decrease.

The concept of economies of scope, related to economies of scale, is particularly relevant for knowledge businesses. Economies of scope exist when a company lowers its unit costs as it pursues a greater variety of activities. A significant example is research-and-development spillovers, in which the ideas that arise in one research project transfer to other projects. Companies that increase the diversification of their research portfolios can often find applications for their ideas better than they could when their research portfolios were smaller.[17]

While economies of scale can be an important source of expectations revisions, our experience suggests that scale benefits often get competed away for all but the leading physical and service companies. Further, some leaders choose to pass on to their customers the benefits of scale by lowering prices to drive sales and market share. For knowledge businesses in winner-take-most markets, size does matter. Because of the demand and cost characteristics of these sectors, first-to-scale advantages can be substantial and often lead to meaningful expectations revisions.

Cost Efficiencies

The two value factors we just explored, operating leverage and economies of scale, depend on sales growth. In contrast, cost efficiency is about lowering costs *independent* of the sales level.

Companies can realize cost efficiencies in two fundamental ways. First, companies can reduce costs within various activities: They do the same thing, but more efficiently. For example, the Kellogg Company, the world's leading producer of ready-to-eat cereal, has been streamlining production and operations to reduce costs.

In its annual report released in early 2000, Kellogg forecast that this program would generate $50 million in pretax savings for 2000 and years thereafter. The company anticipates that its cumulative cost savings, from its 1997–2000 initiatives, will total $245 million (table 9-1). To achieve cost savings, the company had to incur onetime cash outlays exceeding $250 million—to pay for employee retirement and severance programs.

Service companies often replace people with physical infrastructure to effect cost savings. One example is retail banking, where the average cost per transaction has plummeted as customers spend less time interacting with bank tellers and more time using lower-cost automatic teller machines and the Internet (table 9-2). Since these cost savings are available to most large financial institutions, they quickly show up as lowered prices of services. Still, expectations opportunities exist with the adoption leaders and laggards. By staying ahead of the technology curve, first-movers can sustain lower costs than their competition, allowing for higher profitability.

Knowledge companies primarily achieve cost savings by reducing employee head count. Novell, a leading provider of network software, is a case in point. Anticipating annual savings of about $100 million, or 10 percent of sales, in 1997 the company reduced its workforce by approximately 1,000 employees, or 17 percent. In the subsequent two years, sales per employee jumped almost 35 percent.

The second way to realize efficiency is to reconfigure the activities themselves. Consumer products giant Sara Lee Corporation announced a sweeping restructuring plan in the late 1990s. The company's largest business at the time was personal products, mainly Hanes hosiery and knit products. The business was vertically integrated, that is, Sara Lee participated in nearly every phase of the production process.

According to the company's restructuring-related filings, "The key element of this program is a plan to de-verticalize the operations of the corporation to the extent practical and possible." Sara Lee wanted to outsource the non-value-adding operations rather than engage in every step of production. In fact, it sold its U.S. yarn and textile operations soon after its restructuring announcement. Later in the filings, Sara Lee noted that "profits, margins and returns are expected to improve through lower fixed costs and reduced operating costs."[18] Thus the company's goal in reconfiguring its activities was to improve its financial performance, independent of its sales.

TABLE 9-1   Kellogg's Annual Savings from Cost Efficiencies (in Millions of Dollars)

Year	Annual Pretax Savings
1997	$ 60
1998	10
1999	125
2000 expected	50
Total	$245

Source: Kellogg Company.

In sum, expectations opportunities may exist if a company either lowers the cost of performing its activities or reduces costs by reconfiguring the activities themselves. Thus investors should look for companies that have cost structures out of line with the sector, or companies that are especially diligent in their cost-reduction programs (but not at the expense of building value-creating businesses). Cost efficiencies can be an important source in PIE revisions for businesses in all three business categories. But competition often assures that the benefits of cost efficiencies, like economies of scale, are reduced by lower selling prices and other customer benefits.

Investment Efficiencies

Physical companies that allocate investment dollars more efficiently drive higher shareholder value.[19] A company realizes investment efficiencies when it figures out how to generate the same level of after-tax net operating profit for a smaller investment outlay, resulting in higher free cash flow (net operating profit after tax, minus investment) for a given level of sales. The value factor for investment efficiency is, of course, particularly important for capital-intensive businesses.

American Standard, a manufacturer of air conditioning, plumbing, and automotive products, dramatically improved its working-capital efficiency through a technique known as *demand-flow technology*. The basic idea is to pull materials through production based on actual consumer demand rather than a preordained schedule. The program allowed American Standard to save a reported $500 million in working capital.[20] Inventory turns—cost of goods sold divided by inventory—

TABLE 9-2   Average Cost per Transaction in Retail Banking

Channel	Average Cost per Transaction
Branch	$1.14
Telephone	0.55
ATM	0.29
PC banking	0.02
Internet	0.01

Source: Federal Reserve Bank of Dallas.

went from three to nine times during the 1990s. The program was so successful that other leading companies, including General Electric, adopted the techniques.[21]

The world's leading fast-food purveyor, McDonald's, is an illustration of how fixed-capital investment efficiency can add value. Through standardization, global sourcing, and purchasing power, McDonald's trimmed its average U.S. unit development costs significantly in the early 1990s (table 9-3). Notably, expected sales and operating profit margins from these units did not diminish. The improved efficiency translated directly into higher cash flows and shareholder value.

The pattern of investment spending is another important consideration for physical businesses. Companies that compete in cyclical, slow-growth industries often tend to overspend at cyclical peaks and underspend at cyclical troughs. Investors need to monitor investment-spending discipline carefully in these industries. Credit Suisse First Boston's energy analyst, James Clark, found that the integrated oil companies that invested prudently throughout the energy cycle, including Exxon (now Exxon Mobil) and British Petroleum, delivered substantially higher total shareholder returns than those that spent aggressively in the name of growth and market share.[22]

Expectations opportunities are most likely to materialize for companies that change their investment discipline. Tom Copeland shows that manageable reductions in a company's capital-spending budget often create more value than sweeping cuts in payroll do. For example, he estimates that Eastman Kodak Company's 10,000-employee layoff in September 1997—with $400 million in anticipated savings per year—was equivalent to a 14.5 percent cut in its capital spending budget.[23] He

TABLE 9-3   McDonald's Investment per Unit

	1994	1993	1992	1991	1990
Land	$ 317	$ 328	$ 361	$ 433	$ 433
Building	483	482	515	608	720
Equipment	295	317	361	362	403
Average cost	$1,095	$1,127	$1,237	$1,403	$1,556

Source: McDonald's Corporation.
Note: U.S. average development costs, in thousands of dollars.

argues that companies can achieve such cuts without jeopardizing future value-creating investments.

ESSENTIAL IDEAS

- You do not need new rules to understand the sources of value creation across the economic landscape. The basics of expectations investing are sufficiently robust for *all* companies.

- Although the economics of value creation do not change, the characteristics of various business categories—*physical, service,* and *knowledge*—vary.

- Understanding the business categories through the prism of the value factors can help you anticipate expectations revisions.

Part III
reading corporate
signals

10
mergers and
acquisitions

Mergers and acquisitions have become a prominent, and permanent, part of the corporate landscape. In these high-stakes games, companies often risk a substantial percentage of their market capitalization in an effort to improve their competitive positions. And unlike routine capital investments, merger and acquisition (M&A) deals often strike like lightning, literally changing a company's strategic and financial circumstances overnight.

Mergers and acquisitions are significant for investors for several reasons. First, M&A activity is so pervasive that sooner or later it affects a sizable portion of most stock portfolios. Second, no corporate announcement affects the stock price as quickly or as profoundly as a major acquisition. Finally, M&A deals often create buying and selling opportunities that the acquiring and selling company shareholders, as well as other investors, can exploit.

This chapter explores the opportunities and risks that mergers and acquisitions offer investors. We first show how an acquiring company adds value in mergers and acquisitions, including the key issues in evaluating synergies. Next, we lay out the appropriate analytical steps an expectations investor takes on the heels of a deal announcement. These steps include assessing the deal's potential value impact, reading management signals, anticipating the stock market's initial reaction, and updating the analysis after the market's initial reaction.

HOW ACQUIRING COMPANIES ADD VALUE

The most widespread method that investors, investment bankers, companies, and the financial press use to evaluate a merger is the immediate earnings-per-share impact. They view earnings-per-share accretion as good news and earnings-per-share dilution as bad news.

But a narrow focus on a deal's earnings-per-share impact is as dangerous as it is simplistic, because mergers pose an additional problem on top of all the other shortcomings of earnings (chapter 1). An M&A deal can trigger earnings-per-share growth without *any* improvement in the operations of the two companies. In fact, the arithmetic of mergers and acquisitions can generate earnings-per-share growth for the acquirer even while decreasing total earnings for the combined company.

How can such a seeming incongruity occur? Whenever the acquiring company's price-earnings (P/E) multiple is greater than the seller's P/E (including the premium in the purchase price), earnings per share rise. This mathematical axiom says absolutely nothing about value creation.

Consider the salient statistics for the hypothetical companies Buyer Inc., Seller Inc., and the combined company. Prior to the deal, Seller Inc.'s market capitalization stands at $2.8 billion—40 million shares each worth $70. Buyer Inc. offers to exchange one of its shares ($100-per-share market value) for each of Seller Inc.'s shares. This $100-per-share offer represents a $30-per-share premium over Seller Inc.'s current $70-per-share market price. After the merger, 90 million shares will be outstanding—Buyer Inc.'s 50 million of currently outstanding shares plus the 40 million shares it issued to Seller Inc.'s shareholders.

	Buyer Inc.	Seller Inc.	Combined
Price per share	$100	$100*	
Earnings per share	$ 4.00	$ 10.00	$ 6.67
Price-earnings multiple	25	10	
Number of shares (millions)	50	40	90
Total earnings (millions)	$200	$400	$600

*Offer price.

Buyer Inc. currently generates $4.00 of earnings for each of its shares. However, since Buyer Inc. gets $10.00 of earnings for each new share it issues, its earnings per share increase from $4.00 to $6.67 *solely because its P/E is greater than the seller's.* The inverse is also true: If Seller Inc. buys Buyer Inc., it suffers earnings-per-share dilution because of its lower P/E. *In neither case do the earnings per share affect the shareholder-value-added potential of the merger.*

So how do acquirers create value in mergers and acquisitions, if not by adding to earnings per share? They do so by investing at a rate of return greater than the cost of capital. *To determine how much shareholder value the acquiring company will generate, estimate the present value of acquisition benefits or synergies and subtract the acquisition premium.* The premium is the amount in excess of the seller's stand-alone value that the acquirer offers to pay. This formula is simple, but generating synergies is not.[1]

EQUATION 10-1
Value change from an M&A deal = Present value of synergies −
Acquisition premium

The expectations investing process guides your assessment of mergers and acquisitions. Since we know the premium when a deal is announced, our task is to determine whether the synergies are sufficient to add value.[2] Think of it this way: An acquirer is willing to pay a premium to the seller's stand-alone value because the acquirer believes it can generate synergies that exceed that premium. We must assess whether the market will agree with the acquirer.

EVALUATING SYNERGIES

How do we determine what synergies are realistic to expect? First, we turn to management. Companies provide specific guidance on the sources and magnitude of expected synergies in nearly all deals. The degree to which you should count on management's estimate depends largely on its credibility. We find that in many cases, even management's often-optimistic synergy estimate is insufficient to offset the premium.[3] As a result, management's guidance unwittingly triggers an immediate, and warranted, drop in its stock price.

A second way to evaluate synergies is to rely on the expectations infrastructure and the strategic frameworks, developed in chapters 3 and 4, respectively. The expectations infrastructure is an ideal tool for assessing synergies. Logical questions arise as you go from value triggers to value drivers. These include the following:

Sales

- Does the deal lead to a broadened product offering, expanded distribution channels, or improved geographic scope?

- Can the combined company achieve greater operating leverage from investments already made?

- Does the company have an opportunity to capture economies of scale in areas such as raw-material procurement and marketing?

Costs

- Can management eliminate redundant activities, including sales, accounting, legal, and administrative?

Investments

- Does the deal offer asset redeployment opportunities or specific capital management skills that lead to lower long-term investment needs?

Besides these potential operational synergies, an M&A deal may also lead to lower tax and financing costs. While all acquirers enter deals with the best intentions, capturing synergies is clearly a challenge for them. (See sidebar, "The Acquiring Company's Burden.")

WHAT TO DO WHEN A DEAL IS ANNOUNCED

When an M&A deal is announced, you'll want to address a few key questions:

1. Does the deal have material economic consequences for shareholders of the buying and selling companies?

2. Is the buyer sending signals by choosing to pay for the deal with stock instead of cash?

3. What is the stock market's likely initial reaction?

4. How do we update the analysis after the market's initial reaction, but prior to the deal closing?

Answers to these questions will help you identify expectations opportunities that result from merger announcements.

Assessing the Deal's Value Impact: Shareholder Value at Risk

Once companies announce a major M&A deal, both groups of shareholders, as well as other interested investors, need to evaluate how material the deal is likely to be for the shareholders involved.[4] Even if investors do not have enough information to assess the synergies confidently, they must understand the impact on each company's shareholders *if the synergy expectations embedded in the premium fail to materialize.* Rappaport and Sirower present two simple tools for measuring synergy risk—one for the acquirer's shareholders and another for the selling company's shareholders.[5]

The first tool, *shareholder value at risk (SVAR®)* is straightforward and useful for assessing the acquirer's relative synergy risk. Think of it as a "bet your company" index. It shows you what percentage of the acquiring company's value is at risk if the combination doesn't produce any postacquisition synergies.

SVAR for a cash offer is simply the premium divided by the market value of the acquiring firm before the announcement. We can also calculate SVAR by multiplying the premium percentage by the seller's market value relative to the buyer's market value (figure 10-1). The greater the premium percentage that a buyer pays to the seller, and the greater the selling company's market value relative to the acquiring company's market value, the higher the SVAR. Of course, acquirers can lose even more than their premium. In those cases, SVAR underestimates risk.

Let's consider the SVAR numbers for our hypothetical deal. Let's say that Buyer Inc. proposes to pay $4.0 billion ($100 per share) for Seller

THE ACQUIRING COMPANY'S BURDEN

In about two-thirds of all acquisitions that have taken place since the 1980s, the acquirer's stock price falls immediately after the deal is announced.[a] In most cases, that drop is just a precursor of worse to come. The market's routinely negative response to M&A announcements reflects skepticism that the acquirer will be able to maintain the original values of the businesses and also achieve the synergies required to justify the premium. And the evidence shows that the larger the premium, the worse the share-price performance. Why is the market so skeptical? Why do acquiring companies have such a difficult time creating value for their shareholders?

First of all, many acquisitions fail simply because they set the expectations bar too high. Even without the acquisition premium, the prices of both the acquirer and the seller already reflect performance improvements. For example, the current level of operating performance with no assumed improvement accounts for only 20 to 40 percent of the stock price for the 100 largest nonfinancial companies. The ratio is typically much lower for fast-growing technology companies. The rest of the stock price is based entirely on expected improvements to current performance. Viewed in this light, the 30 to 40 percent premium for an acquisition just adds to expectations for significant improvement. What's more, if management diverts important resources from some businesses during postmerger integration, declines in the businesses providing the resources can easily cancel out the performance gains.

Second, acquisitions disappoint because competitors can easily replicate the benefits of the deal. Competitors do not stand idly by while

[a]An acquiring company can structure a fixed-share offer without sending signals that its stock is overvalued. Acquiring companies, for example, often guarantee the seller a minimum price, which protects the seller against a fall in the acquirer's share price below a specified level.

Inc. The premium is \$1.2 billion (\$4.0 billion – \$2.8 billion). Buyer Inc.'s market value is \$5 billion. In a cash deal, Buyer Inc.'s SVAR is \$1.2 billion divided by \$5 billion, or 24 percent. Accordingly, if no synergies materialize, Buyer Inc.'s shares are "at risk" of declining 24 percent.

But Buyer Inc.'s SVAR is lower if it offers Seller Inc.'s shareholders stock instead of cash, because the stock deal transfers some of the risk to

---

an acquirer attempts to generate synergies at their expense. Arguably, unless an acquisition confers a sustainable competitive advantage, it should not command any premium at all. Indeed, acquisitions sometimes increase a company's vulnerability to competitive attack because the demands of integration can divert attention away from competitors. Acquisitions also create an opportunity for competitors to poach talent while organizational uncertainty is high.

Third, although acquisitions are a quick route to growth, they require full payment up front. By contrast, companies make investments in research and development, capacity expansion, or marketing campaigns in stages over time. In acquisitions, the financial clock starts ticking on the entire investment right from the beginning. Not unreasonably, investors want to see compelling evidence of timely performance gains. If they don't, they mark the company's shares down before any integration takes place.

Fourth, all too often the prices of other "comparable" acquisitions, rather than a rigorous assessment of where, when, and how management can accomplish real performance gains, drive the purchase price of an acquisition. Thus, the price may have little to do with achievable value.

Finally, undoing a merger that goes wrong can be difficult and extremely expensive. Managers, with their credibility at stake, may compound the problem by throwing good money after bad in the fleeting hope that more time and money will prove them right. In these cases, merger success is as rare as sightings of Halley's Comet.

Source: Alfred Rappaport and Mark L. Sirower, "Stock or Cash? The Trade-Offs for Buyers and Sellers in Mergers and Acquisitions," *Harvard Business Review*, November—December, 1999, 147–158.

the selling shareholders. To calculate Buyer Inc.'s SVAR for a stock deal, first figure what percentage Buyer Inc.'s shareholders will own in the combined company: 50/(50 + 40) = 55.5 percent. Multiplying that result by the all-cash SVAR of 24 percent gives us a 13.3 percent SVAR for a stock deal.

The magnitude of SVAR is not always obvious, given that deal announcements usually specify terms based only on stock prices (in contrast to premium percentages and relative buyer/seller market value) and deal structures vary. The point is that if SVAR is a relatively small percentage, then the deal is unlikely to have a material *economic* impact on the buyer. In contrast, if SVAR is sizable, then the transaction deserves careful analysis.

We now turn to the second tool, *premium at risk*, a variation of SVAR. Premium at risk is a measure that helps selling shareholders assess their risk if the synergies don't materialize. At issue for sellers is what percentage of the premium is at risk in a *fixed-share offer*, that is, an offer in which the number of shares the buyer will issue is certain. The answer is the percentage of the ownership that the sellers will have in the combined company. In our example, therefore, the premium at

FIGURE 10-1 What Is the Shareholder's Value at Risk (SVAR) in an All-Cash Deal?

RELATIVE MARKET VALUE OF SELLER TO MARKET VALUE OF ACQUIRER

PREMIUM	0.25	0.50	0.75	1.00
30%	7.5%	15%	22.5%	30%
40%	10%	20%	30%	40%
50%	12.5%	25%	37.5%	50%
60%	15%	30%	45%	60%

Source: Reprinted with the permission of The Free Press, a Division of Simon & Schuster, Inc., from *Creating Shareholder Value: A Guide for Managers and Investors*, Revised and Updated by Alfred Rappaport. Copyright © 1986, 1998 by Alfred Rappaport.

risk for Seller Inc.'s shareholders is 44.5 percent. Thus if no synergies materialize, Seller Inc. shareholders receive the $4.0 billion purchase price *minus* 44.5 percent of the $1.2 billion premium, or $3.466 billion. So in a no-synergy scenario, Seller Inc. shareholders receive $86.65 per share ($3.466 billion divided by 40 million) instead of the $100 that the deal announcement suggests.

The premium-at-risk calculation is a rather conservative measure of risk because it assumes that the value of the independent businesses is safe and that only the acquisition premium is at risk. Figure 10-2 presents SVAR and premium at risk for some major stock deals in 1998.

The premium-at-risk calculation shows why a fixed-value offer is more attractive than a fixed-share offer from the seller's perspective. In a *fixed-value offer*, the acquirer does not fix the number of shares it will issue, but rather pledges a value that the sellers will receive at the clos-

FIGURE 10-2   SVAR and Premium at Risk for Major Stock Deals Announced in 1998

Acquirer	Seller	Premium	Relative Market Value of Seller to Acquirer	Cash SVAR	Acquirer's Proportional Ownership	Stock SVAR	Seller's Premium at Risk
McKesson-Robbins	HBO	30%	1.41	42%	37%	16%	63%
Tyco International	AMP	66%	0.18	12%	78%	9%	22%
Halliburton	Dresser Industries	15%	0.58	9%	60%	5%	40%
Household International	Beneficial	82%	1.01	83%	63%	52%	37%
Conseco	Green Tree Financial	83%	0.39	32%	60%	19%	40%
Office Depot International	Viking Office	42%	0.63	26%	63%	16%	37%

ing date. Since the buyer has to issue as many shares as necessary to satisfy that value, its prevailing stock price at closing determines the number of shares it must issue.

If in a fixed-value offer, Buyer Inc.'s stock price falls by the entire pledged premium during the preclosing, then Seller Inc.'s shareholders simply receive additional shares. Since Buyer Inc. completely absorbs Seller Inc.'s premium at risk, Seller Inc.'s price at closing builds in no synergy expectations. Seller Inc.'s shareholders receive not only more shares but also less risky shares. In contrast, in a fixed-share transaction, Seller Inc.'s shareholders bear their proportionate share of any decline in Buyer Inc.'s price from the announcement date on.

Reading Management Signals

An acquiring company's choice of cash or stock often sends a powerful signal to investors. As the SVAR analysis shows, the main distinction between cash and stock is this: In cash transactions, the acquiring shareholders shoulder the entire risk and reward. If the synergies do not materialize, then the acquiring shareholders alone suffer. On the other hand, they capture the entire benefit from synergies that exceed the premium. In stock transactions, buyers and sellers share both the risk and the reward.

So the cash or stock decision sends signals about the acquirer's perceived risks of failing to achieve the expected synergies. We would expect a confident acquirer to pay for the acquisition with cash so that its shareholders would not have to cede any anticipated merger gains to the selling company's shareholders. But if management strongly doubts that the deal will achieve the required level of synergies, we can expect the company to hedge its bets by offering stock. A stock deal reduces the losses of the acquiring company's shareholders by diluting their ownership interest.

Further, if management believes that the market is undervaluing its shares, then it should not issue new shares, because doing so penalizes current shareholders. Research consistently finds that the market takes stock issuance as a sign that management—a group in a position to know about the company's long-term prospects—believes that the stock is overvalued. Ironically, the same CEOs who publicly declare their company's share price to be too low—which suggests that they should use cash for a deal—cheerfully issue heaps of stock at the "too low" price to pay for their acquisitions. Actions speak louder than words: The market responds more favorably to announcements of cash deals than to stock deals.

Stock offers, then, send two potential signals to expectations investors: that the acquiring company's management lacks confidence in the acquisition and that its shares are overvalued.[6] In principle, a company should always proceed with a cash offer if it is confident that it can successfully integrate an acquisition and believes its own shares to be undervalued. A cash offer neatly resolves the valuation problem for acquirers who believe that their shares are undervalued, as well as for sellers who are uncertain about the acquiring company's true value.

Unfortunately, the cash-versus-stock decision is not always so straightforward. For example, a company may not have sufficient cash resources or debt capacity to make a cash offer. In such cases, management may believe that the acquisition is creating value in spite of the additional cost of issuing undervalued shares. Expectations investors therefore cannot treat cash or stock offers as unambiguous signals of the acquirer's prospects.

Research shows that the market responds more favorably when acquirers demonstrate their confidence in the value of their own shares through their willingness to bear more preclosing market risk. A fixed-share offer is not a confident signal, since the seller's compensation drops if the value of the acquirer's shares falls.

A fixed-value offer gives a more confident signal because the sellers receive a stipulated market value while the acquirers bear the entire cost of any decline in their share price before the closing. If the market believes in the offer, then the acquirer's price may even rise, enabling it to issue fewer shares. In that event, the acquiring company's shareholders capture a greater proportion of the deal's value creation.

If you own shares in a company acquired for stock, then you become a partner in the postmerger enterprise. You therefore have as much interest in realizing the synergies as do the shareholders of the acquiring company. If the expected synergies do not materialize, or if other disappointing developments occur after the closing, then you may well lose a significant portion of the premium that the buyer offered.

At the end of the day, selling shareholders should never assume that the announced value in an exchange-of-shares offer is the value they will realize before or after the closing date. Selling early does limit your exposure. But it also carries costs, because the shares of target companies invariably trade below the offer price during the preclosing period (known as an arbitrage spread). Of course, shareholders who intend to wait until after the closing date to sell their shares of the merged company also face uncertainty: They have no way of knowing today what those shares will be worth after the closing. Sell now, and you risk leaving money on the table. Sell later, and you risk downside in the interim.

Anticipating the Stock Market's Initial Reaction

With the basic formula that dictates value change (equation 10-1) and the knowledge of how the cash-versus-stock decision affects buyers and sellers, you have all you need to anticipate the stock market's initial reaction to an M&A announcement.

Start with the M&A value creation equation (equation 10-1). Estimate the present value of synergies—again, management guidance may be helpful—and calculate the premium. Then see table 10-1 to determine the market's likely reaction, based on the deal economics and the cash-versus-stock decision.

Once the stock trades after the announcement, you can impute the synergies that the market expects by simply adding the change in the buyer's market value to the premium. You can then judge the reasonableness of the market's expected synergies. If it appears the market is over- or underestimating synergies, then you may have an investment opportunity.

After the Market's Initial Reaction

The final part of the M&A assessment updates the analysis *after* the deal is announced and the market has reacted. Such analysis enables you to

TABLE 10-1 Gauging the Market's Initial Reaction to an M&A Announcement

	PV Synergies Exceed Premium	PV Synergies Equal Premium	PV Synergies Less Than Premium
Cash			
Buyer's stock price	Up by amount that S > P	No change	Down by amount that S < P
Seller's stock price	Up by premium amount	Up by premium amount	Up by premium amount
Fixed-share stock-for-stock			
Buyer's stock price	Up by (% ownership × amount that S > P)	No change	Down by (% ownership × amount that S < P)
Seller's stock price	Up by premium amount + (% ownership × amount that S > P)	Up by premium amount	Change based on premium − (% ownership × amount that S < P)
Fixed-value stock-for-stock			
Buyer's stock price	Up by amount that S > P	No change	Down by amount that S < P
Seller's stock price	Up by premium amount	Up by premium amount	Up by premium amount

Note: Immediate reaction will not reflect the full premium, because of arbitrage.
Abbreviations: **PV**, present value; **S**, synergies; **P**, premium.

judge the postannouncement attractiveness of the acquirer's and the seller's stock for cash and stock transactions.

Cash offer. Let's start with the implications for a change in the buyer's stock price after a cash offer. Assume, for example, that immediately following the M&A announcement, Buyer Inc.'s stock price declines by 10 percent (from $100 to $90 per share). Buyer Inc.'s shareholders absorbed a portion of the SVAR with this decline. It is a sunk cost. The relevant consideration for shareholders and other investors is what to do *now*. What is important is the *current* synergy risk, which you can determine with a formula that updates the preannouncement SVAR:

EQUATION 10-2

$$\frac{\text{Premium} + \text{Postannouncement market value change}}{\text{Postannouncement market value}} = \text{Current SVAR}$$

Substituting values for our example:

$$\frac{\$1.2 \text{ billion} - \$0.5 \text{ billion}}{\$4.5 \text{ billion}} = 15.6\%$$

The numerator is the sum of the original premium and the change (positive or negative) in Buyer Inc.'s market value; it is therefore the synergy bet that the postannouncement stock price implies. In this case, the numerator is the $1.2 billion premium minus the $0.5 billion market value reduction ($10 stock-price decline multiplied by 50 million shares). The $0.7 billion difference represents the synergy risk that remains for the continuing shareholders of Buyer Inc. or other investors who purchase Buyer Inc. shares at the current price.

The $0.5 billion decline also reduces Buyer Inc.'s market value in the denominator to $4.5 billion. The current SVAR of 15.6 percent is lower than the 24 percent at the time of the announcement because Buyer Inc. shareholders have already absorbed $0.5 billion of the downside risk. Thus the current SVAR reflects the remaining synergy risk for current shareholders and for investors purchasing shares at today's price. Likewise, a favorable market response to the merger announcement increases the SVAR, reflecting the greater risk borne by continuing and new shareholders.

On the other hand, the sellers in a cash transaction assume no synergy risk, because the acquiring shareholders assume all the risk that the expected synergy embedded in the premium will not materialize. The seller, of course, does face one risk: that the buyer will not complete the offer.

Fixed-shares offer. Let's turn to a fixed-shares stock deal. Recall that the SVAR for a stock deal is the all-cash SVAR of 24 percent multiplied by the Buyer Inc.'s postmerger ownership percentage of 55.5 percent, or 13.3 percent. Assume, once again, that upon the announcement of the merger, Buyer Inc.'s stock price falls from $100 to $90 per share. Just as with the cash deal, Buyer Inc.'s shareholders have already borne part of the synergy risk as a consequence of the stock-price decline. The postannouncement SVAR thus falls to 8.6 percent—the postannouncement cash SVAR of 15.6 percent multiplied by the Buyer Inc.'s 55.5 percent postmerger ownership percentage.

The selling shareholders, who will own 44.5 percent of the combined company, have also borne their proportionate share of the fall in Buyer Inc.'s stock price. At Buyer Inc.'s current stock price, only $0.7 billion of the $1.2 billion premium, or 58.3 percent, remains at risk. This 58.3 percent multiplied by Seller Inc.'s 44.5 percent postmerger ownership yields a premium at risk of 26 percent. The question for the selling shareholders is whether they want to risk 26 percent of their premium above and beyond the premium loss they have already sustained.

Fixed-value offer. Finally, let's consider the same circumstances for a fixed-value offer. If Buyer Inc.'s current $90 stock price is also the price at closing, the company will have to issue 44.4 million shares, rather than 40 million shares, to provide the selling shareholders their fixed value of $4.0 billion. As a consequence, Buyer Inc.'s shareholders will own only 53 percent of the combined company. As Buyer Inc.'s shareholders bear the entire risk of its 10 percent postannouncement stock-price decline, the postannouncement SVAR thus falls to 8.2 percent—

the postannouncement cash SVAR of 15.6 percent multiplied by the 53 percent postmerger ownership percentage.

The selling shareholders in a fixed-value offer bear no price risk in the preclosing period. In fact, the more that Buyer Inc.'s stock price falls, the less synergy risk the selling shareholders assume after the closing. With a 10 percent decrease in Buyer Inc.'s stock from $100 to $90, only 58.3 percent of the premium offer ($0.7 billion of the original $1.2 billion) remains at risk. Multiplying that percentage by the selling shareholders' 47 percent stake in the combined company yields a premium at risk of 27.4 percent. Again, the question is whether the selling shareholders want to make a synergy bet with over a quarter of their premium at risk.

Mergers and acquisitions provide a fertile source of potential expectations opportunities for investors who can read management signals and assess the economic consequences. Further, although splashy M&A announcements may quickly fade from many investors' minds, the tools we've presented in this chapter allow you to analyze a deal's implications both upon announcement and during the postannouncement period.

ESSENTIAL IDEAS

- Earnings-per-share changes are a poor proxy for M&A success.

- The shareholder value added by the acquiring company is equal to the present value of synergies minus the premium.

- Shareholder value at risk (SVAR) shows acquiring shareholders what percentage of their stock price they are betting on the success of the acquisition.

- The premium at risk shows the selling shareholders what percentage of their premium they are betting on the success of the acquisition.

- In cash acquisitions, the acquiring shareholders assume the entire synergy risk, whereas in stock transactions, the selling shareholders share it.

- A stock deal sends two potential signals to expectations investors: that management lacks confidence in the acquisition and that the acquiring company's shares are overvalued.

- Postannouncement price changes in the acquirer's stock require a recalculation of SVAR to identify possible buying and selling opportunities.

11

share buybacks

The popularity of share buybacks has catapulted since the early 1980s. In the United States alone, corporate expenditures on share buybacks as a percentage of earnings were ten times higher in the late 1990s than they were in 1980. In the late 1990s, for the first time, companies spent more money repurchasing their shares than paying dividends.[1] Share buybacks are also flourishing globally. In recent years, countries like the United Kingdom and Canada have seen an increase in activity while other nations that previously prohibited buybacks, including Germany and Japan, have adopted provisions to make them acceptable. Notwithstanding this surge in popularity (table 11-1), the impact of buybacks on shareholder value—and hence on the expectations investor—has never been more ambiguous.

Under the right circumstances, buybacks provide expectations investors a signal to revise their expectations about a company's prospects. Indeed, share buybacks are a very effective way for managers to increase their company's share price when they have more bullish beliefs about their company's prospects than investors do. The signal, however, is not always clear. Buybacks serve a crosscurrent of interests, which can leave investors with little if any trace of a meaningful signal.

In this chapter, we develop guidelines for evaluating share-buyback programs. We start with our primary interest: to identify when buyback announcements offer a credible signal to revise expectations. We go on to present a golden rule that we can use to evaluate all buyback programs. Finally, we apply the golden rule as a benchmark to evaluate the most popularly cited reasons for share buybacks.

So what should you do when a company announces a share-buyback program? First, you must decide whether management is providing a credible signal that the market should revise its expectations. Just as expectations investors find reasons to revise their expectations, so too do corporate managers.

If management sends a credible signal that investors need to revise their expectations, then you need to revisit the expectations investing process (chapters 5–7). A positive signal conveys management's convic-

TABLE 11-1   Market Value of U.S. Share Repurchase Announcements (in Millions of Dollars)

Year	Dutch Auctions	Tender Offers	Open Market	Total
1980	$ —	$ 5	$ 1,429	$ 1,434
1981	—	1,329	3,013	4,342
1982	—	1,164	3,112	4,276
1983	—	1,352	2,278	3,630
1984	9	10,517	14,910	25,436
1985	1,123	13,352	22,786	37,261
1986	2,332	5,492	28,417	36,241
1987	1,502	4,764	34,787	41,053
1988	7,695	3,826	33,150	44,671
1989	5,044	1,939	62,873	69,856
1990	1,933	3,463	39,733	45,129
1991	739	4,715	16,139	21,593
1992	1,638	1,488	32,635	35,761
1993	1,291	1,094	35,000	37,385
1994	925	2,796	71,036	74,757
1995	969	542	81,591	83,102
1996	2,774	2,562	157,917	163,253
1997	5,442	2,552	163,688	171,682
1998	2,640	4,364	215,012	222,016
1999	3,817	1,790	137,015	142,622
Total	$39,873	$69,106	$1,156,521	$1,265,500

Source: Gustavo Grullon and David L. Ikenberry, "What Do We Know About Stock Repurchases?" *Journal of Applied Corporate Finance* (Spring 2000): 31. Reprinted with permission.

tion that expectations about consensus value drivers are too low. And one of the surest ways for a company's managers to create value for its continuing shareholders is to repurchase stock from shareholders who do not accept management's more optimistic view.[2]

If management signals that its stock is undervalued, then you must determine which of the value driver expectations are too low. We recommend revisiting the expectations infrastructure as a systematic way to unearth the source of the revision. As a guide, consider the following items:

- *Sales:* volume, price and mix, operating leverage, economies of scale

- *Costs:* cost efficiency

- *Investments:* working- and fixed-capital spending efficiency

- *Capital structure:* mix of debt and equity financing

Notice that we added capital structure. Companies sometimes use share buybacks to increase their financial leverage, which investors often construe favorably because it suggests confidence in future cash flows. An increase in contractually obligated interest payments also limits a company's ability to reinvest excess cash at a rate below the cost of capital. So financial leverage can reduce so-called agency costs—the misalignment of management and shareholder interests.[3]

When is a buyback program a negative signal? It is a negative sign in at least two cases. The first is when a buyback indicates that management has run out of value-creating projects. When a company would rather return cash to its shareholders than invest in its business, you can infer that the market's expectations for the company's value-creating opportunities are too high. The second case is when management repurchases stock to achieve announced earnings-per-share targets. In other words, since the company's operational performance is coming up short, it turns to financial engineering to achieve its objectives.

THE GOLDEN RULE OF SHARE BUYBACKS

We've developed a golden rule of share buybacks, which you can use as a universal yardstick for evaluating the economic attractiveness of buyback programs:

A company should repurchase its shares only when its stock is trading below its expected value and when no better investment opportunities are available.

Let's dissect this rule. The first part—"a company should repurchase its shares only when its stock is trading below its expected value"—is fully consistent with the expectations investing process. In effect, management is a good investor when it buys its shares when price is lower than value. And if management's assessment of expected value is reasonable (that is, if price is truly less than value), then wealth transfers from exiting shareholders to continuing shareholders. As a result, the expected value per share for the continuing holders increases, which jibes with the notion that management's objective is to maximize shareholder value for its continuing shareholders.

The second part—"no better investment opportunities are available"—addresses a company's priorities. Buybacks may appear attractive, but reinvesting in the business may be a better opportunity. Value-maximizing companies fund the highest-return investments first.

The golden rule also has two noteworthy corollaries:

- *The rate of return from a buyback depends on how much the market is undervaluing the stock.* If a company's shares trade below its expected value and exiting shareholders are willing to sell at that price, then continuing shareholders will earn a return in excess of the cost of equity. The greater the undervaluation, the higher the return to continuing shareholders.[4] The shareholder rate of return—the return that continuing shareholders can expect—equals the cost of equity capital divided by the ratio of stock price to expected value.[5] For example, say that a company has a 10 percent cost of equity and is trading at 80 percent of expected value. Dividing 10 percent by 80 percent gives a 12.5 percent rate of return for the continuing shareholders. Managers and investors can compare this return with alternative investments and rank its relative attractiveness. This formula also shows that buybacks above expected value generate returns below the cost of equity.

- *A buyback can be more attractive than an investment in the business.* Shareholder-value-oriented management teams understand that they should fund all investments that promise to create value. But what if a company has no excess cash or borrowing capacity and, to finance a prospective share buyback, must partially or wholly forgo value-creating investments in the business? A company should consider a share buyback only when its expected return is greater than the expected return from investing in the business.[6]

We now have a way to assess management's share-buyback decision. But even if management has all the right intentions, we must judge whether it has based its decisions on a proper understanding of the market's expectations. Beware, too, of management overconfidence. Managers almost always believe that the shares of their company are undervalued, and they rarely have a full understanding of the expectations embedded in their stock.[7] History is littered with companies that bought back "undervalued" shares only to see business prospects deteriorate and their stocks plummet.

FOUR POPULAR MOTIVATIONS FOR SHARE BUYBACKS

We now look at the four primary reasons that companies cite for buying back their stock. In particular, we want to separate the wheat from the chaff: the decisions that benefit continuing shareholders from those that do not—including decisions that actually harm continuing shareholders. We are looking for signals, with the golden rule as our guide. Wherever companies violate the rule, we'll explain management's apparent rationale.

1. To Signal the Market That Shares Are Undervalued

Even though this reason—the signaling that shares are undervalued—is the one that companies cite most often, the signal has become weaker in recent years. Why?

To start, an announced buyback suffers from what we call the politician's-pledge problem. In an effort to curry voter favor, politicians often promise tax cuts but remain notoriously vague about the magnitude and timing of the tax relief. Likewise, companies often announce buybacks, but they do not always follow through. In fact, companies fail to complete about 25 percent of authorized open-market buyback programs within three years of the announcement.[8] Just as voters are wary of the politician's pledge, investors realize that an announced program is not the same as a completed program.

Another reason that the buyback signal is weaker relates to the three methods that companies use to buy back their shares:

- *Open-market purchases.* In this buyback method, the most widely used by far, companies simply repurchase their own shares in the open market, as any other investor would. Although open-market purchases have legal restrictions—such as a limit to the daily volume that a company can purchase—this method offers the company the greatest degree of flexibility. On the other hand, open-market purchases convey the weakest signal of management conviction, particularly when these purchases merely offset the dilution from employee stock options.

- *Dutch auction.* In a Dutch auction, management defines the number of shares it intends to buy, an expiration date, and a price range (generally a premium to the market) within which it is willing to buy. Shareholders may tender their shares at any price within the range. Starting at the bottom of the range, the company sums the cumulative number of shares necessary to fulfill the program. All tendering shareholders at or below the "clearing price" receive the clearing price for their stock. Dutch auctions are generally strong signals, and management can execute them relatively efficiently.[9]

- *Fixed-price tender offers.* With this buyback method, management offers to repurchase a set number of shares at a fixed price through an expiration date. The price is often a significant premium to the market price, and companies generally tender for a sizable percentage of the shares outstanding. Shareholders may or may not elect to tender their shares. Fixed-price tenders, especially debt-financed ones, tend to be powerful, positive signals to the market.[10]

Open-market purchases emit the weakest signal, whereas Dutch auctions and fixed-price tenders tend to convey decidedly stronger signals. In the late 1980s, Dutch auctions and fixed-price tenders represented about 21 percent of announced buyback volume in the United States. In the 1990s, however, they constituted only 5 percent of the total. Consequently, the relative number of strong-signal announcements is down sharply.

The circumstances that surround a buyback also affect the interpretation of the signal. In particular, a few factors point to the strength of management's conviction that the shares are undervalued:[11]

- *Size of buyback program.* All things being equal, the larger the program—the higher percentage of the float that a company retires—the greater management's conviction.

- *Premium to market price.* Sizable premiums reflect not only a belief that expectations are too low, but also a willingness to act on such conviction.

- *Insider ownership.* Relatively high insider ownership better aligns the economic interests of managers and shareholders. Managers with relatively significant equity stakes are more likely to invest only in value-creating opportunities than to maximize the size of the company.

- *Insider selling.* When managers execute a sizable buyback program and indicate that they will not sell any of their shares, they are increasing their personal bet on the success of the company. This action sends a positive message to the market.

As the previous situations show, to determine whether management is sending a credible undervaluation signal, you must heed the age-old adage "actions speak louder than words." Open-market buyback announcements with vague terms rarely if ever signal the need to revise expectations. In these cases, you should assess whether other factors motivate management. On the other hand, significant revisions in expectations are likely to accompany large Dutch auctions or fixed-price tenders, especially those at a substantial premium to the market. Even here, you must decide whether management's decision-making process incorporates price-implied expectations.

2. To Manage Earnings per Share

When management announces a share buyback for the purpose of managing earnings per share, management actions and the golden rule of share buybacks often come into direct conflict. Earnings per share do not explain value well, because they do not incorporate the cost of capital, they neglect investment needs, and they can be computed using alternative accounting methods (chapter 1).

Nevertheless, management teams persist in their efforts to maximize short-term earnings per share—sometimes, as we will see, at the expense of maximizing shareholder value. Why? First, they believe that the investment community mechanically and uncritically applies a multiple to current earnings to establish value. Given the persuasive evidence that the market impounds expectations for long-term cash flows, this view is questionable. Second, many executive compensation schemes are still partially tied to earnings targets. Although stock options dominate incentive compensation, managers sometimes forgo long-term value creation in the name of the short-term earnings game.

Share buybacks facilitate earnings management in two ways. First, some buyback programs seek to offset the earnings-per-share dilution from employee stock option (ESO) programs. In this case, companies aim to buy enough shares to keep the level of outstanding shares constant. The rate of ESO exercise and prevailing market prices dictate the magnitude and price of the buybacks.[12]

This motivation for a buyback program has no sound financial basis. It clearly risks violating the buyback golden rule if the company's stock price is not below its expected value or if better opportunities exist to invest in the business. Companies that buy back stock to offset ESO dilution may unwittingly reduce the value of the continuing shareholders' holdings.

Companies also use share buybacks a second way: to boost earnings per share. The *Wall Street Journal* repeats this supposed benefit, almost by rote, nearly every time a company announces a noteworthy buyback program. Here is a typical quote: "The appeal behind share repurchases is . . . fairly straightforward. A company buys up a portion of its shares outstanding, which gives a boost to its earnings-per-share figures."[13]

This statement is not even mathematically correct, let alone economically sensible.

Whether a buyback program increases or decreases earnings per share is a function of the price/earnings (P/E) multiple and either (1) the company's forgone after-tax interest income or (2) the after-tax cost of new debt used to finance the buyback. More specifically, when the inverse of the price-earnings multiple $[1/(P/E) = E/P]$ is lower than the after-tax interest rate, a buyback adds to earnings per share. When E/P is greater than the after-tax interest rate, a buyback reduces earnings per share. But we would be wrong to judge the merits of an investment, including a buyback, by its immediate impact on earnings per share.

Here's an example. Assume that three companies (A, B, and C) have identical $100 cash balances, operating income, tax rates, shares outstanding, and earnings per share. Only their stock prices are different (table 11-2).

We assume that each company uses its $100 cash balance to buy back its shares.[14] A, B, and C can buy ten, three, and two shares, respectively. We now see that earnings per share increase for Company A, do not change for Company B, and decline for Company C (table 11-3). Note that the changes in earnings per share are completely independent of the relationship between stock price and expected value. A buyback of an overvalued stock can add to earnings per share while

TABLE 11-2   Company Comparison prior to Share Buyback

	Company A	Company B	Company C
Operating income	$ 95	$ 95	$ 95
Interest income ($100 at 5%)	$ 5	$ 5	$ 5
Pretax income	$100	$100	$100
Taxes (at 40%)	$ 40	$ 40	$ 40
Net income	$ 60	$ 60	$ 60
Shares outstanding	60	60	60
Earnings per share	**$ 1.00**	**$ 1.00**	**$ 1.00**
Stock price	$ 10.00	$ 33.00	$ 50.00
P/E	10.0	33.3	50.0
E/P	10.0%	3.0%	2.0%
After-tax interest rate	3.0%	3.0%	3.0%

decreasing the value of the continuing shareholders' investment, and a buyback of an undervalued stock can reduce earnings per share while increasing the value of the continuing shareholders' stake in the company.

Thus earnings-per-share accretion or dilution has nothing to do with whether a buyback makes economic sense, because the relationship between the P/E and interest income (or expense) dictates the earnings-per-share accretion or dilution, whereas the relationship between stock price and expected value dictates a buyback's economic merits. And since earnings and P/E are so unreliably linked to expected value—as chapter 1 demonstrates—they are of no use in judging the attractiveness of a buyback program.

Repurchasing overvalued shares—or refraining from buying undervalued shares—because of an unfavorable earnings-per-share impact is shareholder-unfriendly finance. Similarly, the notion that buybacks of high-P/E stocks are bad, or that buybacks of low-P/E stocks are good, defies economic reasoning. Expectations investors should always apply the price-to-expected-value standard, and be wary of companies that buy back their stock primarily, or solely, to boost earnings per share. If you own shares of companies with such a short-term orientation, you may want to consider whether market expectations are unduly optimistic and whether you should sell the shares.

3. To Return Cash to Shareholders Efficiently

Companies have two basic choices when they want to return cash to shareholders: to pay a dividend or to buy back their stock. As we will

TABLE 11-3   Company Comparison after Share Buyback

	Company A	Company B	Company C
Operating income	$95	$95	$95
Interest income	$ 0	$ 0	$ 0
Pretax income	$95	$95	$95
Taxes (at 40%)	$38	$38	$38
Net income	$57	$57	$57
Shares outstanding	50	57	58
Earnings per share	**$ 1.14**	**$ 1.00**	**$ 0.98**

see, the preferred method depends on several conditions, most notably taxes and the stock-price-to-expected-value relationship.

That said, dividends are in clear demise. For example, although two-thirds of U.S. companies paid a dividend in 1978, only about one-fifth did so in the late 1990s.[15] Since the mid-1980s, a majority of firms have chosen to initiate cash payments to their shareholders through share buybacks rather than through dividends. And while many large, established firms have not cut their dividends, evidence shows that they are financing their share-buyback programs with funds that they otherwise would have used to boost dividends.

As an expectations investor, you should care about how companies return cash to shareholders for two reasons. First, you must consider the role of taxes. Share buybacks are generally more tax efficient than dividends. Second, buybacks that occur at prices higher than expected value may reduce shareholder value for continuing shareholders.

Let's look at taxes first. Share buybacks are a more tax-efficient means of returning cash to taxable investors than dividends, for the following reasons:[16]

- *Tax-rate differential.* Tax rates for ordinary income differ significantly from those for capital gains. Dividends are taxed at the ordinary income-tax rate—currently as high as 39.6 percent. In contrast, the tax for long-term capital gains is 20 percent, roughly half the highest ordinary income rate. Yet even this differential understates the after-tax benefits of buybacks. Specifically, shareholders who want a cash "yield" similar to a dividend yield can sell a portion of their holdings, but pay only capital-gains taxes on the difference between the selling price and their cost. In contrast, the full amount of a dividend is taxable.

- *Time is on your side.* Another tax advantage to buybacks is deferral. Shareholders can choose to retain rather than tender their stock and defer tax payments until they sell. Thus buybacks are more advantageous than dividends not only because of the lower tax *rate*, but also because of the discretionary *timing* for incurring the tax liability.

These tax issues, while important, do not fully explain the decline of dividend yields. Eugene Fama and Kenneth French note that part of the decline reflects the changing characteristics of publicly traded firms. A strong market for initial public offerings has tilted the population of traded companies more toward small firms with limited profitability but good growth prospects. These firms are far less likely to pay dividends.

The sharp increase in ESO programs has also blunted dividends. Since ESO holders do not typically receive dividends, the value of their options decreases when their companies pay dividends.[17] Not surprisingly, managers in options-laden companies have little incentive to pay dividends.

The relative tax efficiency of buybacks notwithstanding, expectations investors must keep in mind the golden rule of share buybacks. When the stock price exceeds its expected value, buybacks transfer value from the continuing to the selling shareholders. And even if buybacks are more tax efficient than dividends, you should always ask whether you might find better alternatives for investing the cash in the business.

4. To Increase Financial Leverage

Share buybacks are an effective way for underleveraged firms to increase their debt/equity ratio. Since a significant change in a company's capital structure can affect shareholder value, such changes should interest expectations investors. An appropriate level of financial leverage provides a balance between the benefits of interest-expense tax shields and the risk of financial distress.

For profitable companies, tax-deductible interest expense creates a valuable tax shield. If it is reasonable to assume a permanent change in capital structure, then you can estimate the value of the tax shield by capitalizing the tax savings. Simply divide the tax savings (interest expense multiplied by marginal tax rate) by the pretax cost of debt.[18]

At a certain point, the risks of financial distress outweigh the benefits of debt. A company with too much debt may not be able to meet its contractual commitments. Financial distress is onerous, involving substantial direct costs, such as legal and administrative bankruptcy fees, and indirect costs, such as the loss of customers and suppliers. Stock buybacks that increase financial leverage can lead to a legitimate, albeit generally onetime, increase in shareholder value. As an expectations investor, however, you should not lose sight of the fundamental price-to-value relationship. In other words, if a company's stock price exceeds its expected value, the company can probably find less costly ways to increase financial leverage.

Expectations investors are always alert to signals of potential expectations revisions. Share buybacks offer a prime source for such signals. But you must evaluate share buybacks critically, because the potency of the signal—if it exists at all—is harder to detect today than ever before. Indeed, many companies are buying back their shares for reasons that do not stand up to economic scrutiny. The golden rule of share buybacks is the most reliable guide for assessing the merits of any buyback announcement.

ESSENTIAL IDEAS

- Share buybacks were much more prominent by the year 2000 than they were twenty years before.

- Buybacks can be a prime signal that investors need to revise expectations for a company's value drivers.

- You can rely on the following golden rule to measure all buyback announcements: A company should repurchase its shares only when its stock is trading below its expected value and when no better investment opportunities are available.

- Companies cite four primary reasons for buying back stock:

    1. To signal the market that shares are undervalued

    2. To manage earnings per share

    3. To return cash to shareholders efficiently

    4. To increase financial leverage

- Investors must critically assess management's motivation for buying back stock. Managers often serve interests other than those of their continuing shareholders.

12
incentive
compensation

In business, as in many facets of life, incentives play a large role in determining subsequent performance. And since the expectations for future financial performance lie at the heart of expectations investing, a company's incentive compensation arrangements should concern us as investors. While most investors readily acknowledge the significant interplay between incentive compensation and performance, many fail to appreciate that a company's management incentives can provide important clues about likely upward and downward expectations revisions.[1]

Three issues in particular stand out. First, investors assume that as long as companies offer equity-linked compensation (predominately employee stock options, or ESOs), managers have the appropriate incentives to generate superior returns—that is, returns that exceed an appropriate benchmark. As we will show, many incentive compensation schemes—including equity-linked schemes—are essentially pay-delivery mechanisms rather than true incentives.

Second, investors believe that ESOs are the right compensation tool for all levels of management. In fact, options are not the right compensation tool for employees who have little practical control over stock-price performance. This group, of course, includes most employees.

Finally, most ESO programs provide too much compensation when the stock market is strong and too little when markets are weak. As a result, executives often simply reprice (or reissue) options after a market decline. This situation presents shareholders with an unsatisfactory heads-I-win, tails-you-lose proposition.

In this chapter, we discuss properly designed performance measures and compensation arrangements. The objective of an incentive system is unambiguous—to motivate managers and employees to create value by rewarding them for the value that they create. The best incentive programs encourage managers to deliver results that exceed market expectations. Ill-conceived programs reward mediocrity, and they are often the precursor to disappointing financial results.

Almost all companies proudly proclaim their dedication to increasing shareholder value. But in practice many companies base their incentive compensation plans on a wide range of performance standards, each affecting managers' behavior in different ways.

Typically, companies develop performance standards for incentive pay at three levels: (1) the CEO and other corporate-level executives, (2) operating-unit executives, and (3) middle managers and frontline employees. For each level, you should ask two basic questions:

- Is the company using an appropriate *measure* of performance?

- Is the company targeting an appropriate threshold *level* of performance?

CEO AND OTHER CORPORATE-LEVEL EXECUTIVES

The primary responsibility of the CEO and other senior corporate executives is to maximize long-term total shareholder returns. Exceptional management teams strive for and achieve superior shareholder returns over a sustained period. Shareholders rightfully expect boards of directors to establish performance standards and incentive compensation arrangements that motivate management to deliver these returns.

Corporate-level executives, starting with the CEO, typically receive salary, short- and long-term bonuses (based on achieving financial targets), and ESOs. The link between bonuses and superior shareholder returns is usually tenuous at best, particularly in companies whose short-term financial performance dominates bonus payments. Stock options, on the other hand, directly link to shareholder returns. As we will see, however, standard stock-option plans can reward performance well below superior-return levels.

In the early 1990s, corporate boards began to focus on shareholder value and became convinced that the surest way to align the interests of managers and shareholders was to make stock options a large component of compensation. A decade later, stock options accounted for more than half of total CEO compensation in the largest U.S. companies and for about 30 percent of senior operating executive pay. Options and stock grants also constituted almost half the remuneration for directors.

But standard stock-options programs miss the pay-for-performance mark. In a bull market, the conventional stock option rewards even mediocre performance. That's because executives profit from *any* increase in share price—even one well below what competitors or the overall market realize.[2] And since bull markets are fueled not only by corporate performance but also by factors beyond management control, such as lower interest rates, executives enjoy huge windfalls simply by being in the right place at the right time. For example, L.E.K. Consulting analyzed the stock options granted to the CEOs of the companies in the Dow Jones Industrial Average between 1993 and 1998. For the companies in this group, L.E.K. could attribute only 40 percent of the increase in option value to performance above the average of their respective industry, and only 32 percent for performance beyond that of the Standard & Poor's 500.

On the other side of the coin, executives who outperform their peers in down markets lose out. With standard option packages, bear markets overshadow superior performance and cause executives to lose wealth precisely when they provide the best relative results. Both the free ride in a bull market and an undue penalty in a bear market undermine the objectives of an appropriate pay-for-superior-performance system.

Although CEOs consistently acknowledge the paramount importance of delivering superior returns to shareholders, we must recognize, as expectations investors, that standard stock-option plans do not distinguish between below-average and superior performance. In other words, boards are not setting the right *level* of required performance for incentive pay. Before we review an alternative option plan that does tie rewards to superior performance, let's look briefly at how companies grant options under existing plans and the implications for investors.

Brian Hall divides the ways that companies grant options into three categories:[3]

- *Fixed-value plans,* which offer executives a predetermined annual value over the plan period

- *Fixed-number plans,* which stipulate the number of options that executives receive annually over the plan period

- *Megagrants,* which are large, up-front grants offered in lieu of annual grants

With fixed-value plans, a company is less likely to lose executives because the plans assure new options in the succeeding year even if the stock price falls. These plans insulate annual grants from the company's performance because executives receive *more* options if the stock price falls and *fewer* options if the stock price increases. Fixed-value plans, while popular, provide the weakest incentives of the three types of programs. You should be particularly concerned when you find fixed-value plans in static companies whose executives lack entrepreneurial drive. In such situations do not look for expectations to be revised upward. More likely, management will end up with a larger piece of the company while shareholders bear the cost of sustained underperformance.

Fixed-number plans offer a stronger pay-for-performance link than do fixed-value plans because the value of the annual at-the-money options increases as the stock price rises.[4] Likewise, a fall in the stock price decreases the value of future option grants. With fixed-number plans, a company risks losing executives, since the value of the prespecified number of shares is smaller if the stock price falls.

Megagrants provide the most powerful value-creation incentive for executives because both the number of options and the exercise price are fixed in advance. In other words, these grants provide executives with contingent equity years in advance of hoped-for performance. Although companies do not offer megagrant plans as frequently as they offer multiyear plans, megagrants are common in Silicon Valley high-technology companies.

Although megagrants provide a strong incentive to executives at the time of the grant, the incentive quickly erodes if the stock price drops and the options fall significantly below the exercise price. Megagrants are particularly risky for high-technology start-ups with volatile stock prices because retaining executives with underwater megagrants is very difficult in a tight labor market. Ironically, the most frequent users of megagrants, high-technology start-ups, are precisely those most likely to suffer employee turnover as a consequence of a falling stock price.

How does all this information fit into your expectations analysis? First, determine which approach a company uses to grant options. Then assess the trade-off between the strength of the incentive and the risk of losing executives. *A mismatch between the options-grant approach and the company's circumstances may signal that you should lower your expectations estimates or establish a higher probability for your worst-case scenario.*

Can companies eliminate most of the limitations of standard stock-option grants? Yes. In fact, companies can design relatively straightforward option programs that reward exceptional performers with greater gains than they would achieve with standard options, while appropriately penalizing poor performers. Expectations investors should be alert to companies that adopt such a program and should advocate its implementation when possible.

An *indexed-option* program best aligns the interests of managers and shareholders seeking superior returns.[5] With this kind of option, the exercise price that executives pay is tied either to an index of the company's competitors or to a broader market index. For example, if the chosen index increases by 20 percent, then the exercise price of the options increases by the same percentage. The indexed options in this case are worth exercising only if the company's shares rise more than 20 percent, outperforming the index.

Indexed options do not reward underperforming executives simply because the market is rising. Nor do they penalize superior performers because the market is steady or declining. If the index declines, then so does the exercise price, which keeps executives motivated even in a sustained bear market. Significantly, indexed options reward superior performance in all markets.

Despite their appeal and the support of notables such as Federal Reserve Chairman Alan Greenspan and a growing chorus of institutional investors, indexed options remain a rare species.[6] CEOs shun them because they inject more risk into their compensation packages. Companies express additional concerns. For one thing, accounting rules penalize companies for using indexed options. Unlike standard options, companies must reflect the annual cost of indexed options on their income statement. For another thing, companies have to grant more indexed options than conventional options to provide a comparable initial value, and shareholders therefore suffer from "too much dilution."

Both concerns are misplaced. In the first case, the cost to shareholders is the same, whether a company charges option costs as an expense or whether it discloses the cost in a footnote to the financial statements.

TO REPRICE OR NOT TO REPRICE

After a period of poor stock-price performance, which causes the value of ESOs to evaporate, a company faces tough decisions. In particular, it must decide whether to reprice (lower) the exercise price of existing options or to exchange them for newer options with more favorable terms. How should an expectations investor view this decision?

In essence, the decision is a difficult trade-off. If the company doesn't reprice and can't afford to increase cash compensation, it risks losing the very lifeblood of its value creation: key employees. A company's ability to recruit, motivate, and retain key employees in a highly competitive labor market when its stock options are hopelessly underwater is difficult, to say the least, and it is symptomatic of negative reflexivity, that is, a negative feedback loop. (See chapter 8 for a discussion of reflexivity.)

If the company does reprice, on the other hand, it risks institutionalizing a pay delivery system, thus subverting the spirit and objectives of an incentive compensation program. This initiative effectively rewrites the rules in midstream.

A sensible solution exists: replacing the underwater options with indexed

The second concern, too, defies economic logic. Worries over dilution should not dwell on the number of options granted, but rather on the number that executives can exercise in the absence of superior performance. Because standard option plans can reward executives for below-average performance, they always pose a greater risk of economic dilution than do indexed-option plans.

OPERATING-UNIT EXECUTIVES

Although CEO pay draws the headlines, the compensation of operating executives receives far less scrutiny even though it is equally critical to the success of public companies. After all, a company's operating units are its primary source of value. In decentralized companies with a range of products and markets, operating executives make the important day-to-day operating and investment decisions. The way that the CEO evaluates and pays these operating-unit executives affects their behavior

options, which is a win-win program for shareholders and managers. It delights shareholders because executives have a powerful economic incentive to create superior shareholder value. Furthermore, shareholders are pleased to pay generously for superior performance while withholding rewards for mediocre performance. CEOs and other executives should be equally delighted and energized by the possibility of earning significant option profits under any stock market condition.[a] Not only do indexed options provide corporate boards a solution to the problem of underwater options, but they also offer the fundamental reform needed to link incentive pay with the goal of investors—achieving superior performance.

[a]How many indexed options should a company grant for each existing conventional option? The answer depends on how far the company's stock price has fallen below the exercise price for existing options. As options move increasingly underwater, they become less valuable; therefore a company needs fewer indexed options for an even-value exchange. Take, as an example, a company with an $80 stock price and exercise price of $100 per share. As calculated by option-pricing models, the estimated values of the 20 percent underwater option and an at-the-market indexed option are virtually identical. To entice reluctant executives in this particular situation, the board might offer a premium exchange rate of, say, 1.25 or even 1.50 indexed options for each existing option.

and, ultimately, operating results. Just as investors scrutinize CEO compensation, they should determine whether the company has properly aligned the performance targets and incentive pay for operating-unit executives with the interests of shareholders.

Stock options, along with annual and long-term financial incentives, account for well over half the compensation for operating executives. Unfortunately, option plans and financial targets are often inappropriate incentives. A company's stock price is not an appropriate performance measure for an individual operating unit. Such units are essentially private companies embedded in publicly traded companies. Operating-unit executives usually have a limited impact on the company's overall success and hence its stock price. Incentives based on the share price do not give them the rewards they deserve.

A stock price that declines because of disappointing performance in other parts of the company may unfairly penalize the executives of the superior-performing operating unit. Alternatively, if an operating unit performs poorly but the company's shares rise because of superior performance by other units, the executives of that unit will enjoy an unearned windfall. Only when a company's operating units are truly interdependent can the share price be a fair and useful guide to operating performance.

Companies frequently use financial measures such as operating income and return on invested capital to measure operating-unit performance. These measures do not reliably link to shareholder value, however. To overcome the criticism that measures of earnings do not incorporate the cost of capital, a growing number of companies deduct a cost-of-capital charge from earnings. While some consultants and managers purport that the resulting "residual-income" calculation is a reasonable estimate of shareholder value added, residual income remains essentially an earnings number with all its shortcomings.[7] Even if residual income were a reasonable measure of performance, companies frequently set the level of minimum acceptable performance too low.

Management creates value when the returns on incremental corporate investments exceed the cost of capital. But that does not mean that an incentive system should reward operating executives for *any* value creation. *Companies that use the cost-of-capital standard as a threshold*

for incentive compensation generally ignore the expectations of value cre-
ation that a company's stock price already implies.

Take a company with a 10 percent cost of capital. Say that the share
price reflects the market's belief that the company will find opportunities to invest at an average expected rate of return of 25 percent. If managers start to invest in projects yielding less, say 15 percent, then
investors will revise their expectations downward and the company's
stock price will fall. Few would argue that the company should reward
managers for such performance, even though they beat the cost of
capital.

How then should the company set incentive pay for an operating
unit? To deliver superior returns to its shareholders, a company's operating units must collectively deliver value that exceeds the level implied
by the current stock price. The CEO and other corporate-level executives are unlikely to profit from their indexed options if performance
falls below that level. Compensation schemes should therefore reward
operating executives for delivering *superior shareholder value added*
(SSVA®).[8]

If a company uses the wrong measure of performance or an inappropriate level of threshold performance, then investors have good reason to question how well the incentives in place motivate superior value
creation. This concern, in turn, should make investors more cautious
when they assess the likelihood of favorable expectations revisions.

MIDDLE MANAGERS AND FRONTLINE EMPLOYEES

A company needs appropriate incentive pay measures at every level to
maximize its potential for superior returns. Establishing measures that
can guide hands-on decision making by frontline employees is the final
piece of the puzzle. Superior shareholder value added and supporting
value drivers such as sales growth and operating profit margins are too
broad to provide much day-to-day guidance. Middle managers and
frontline employees need to know what specific actions they can take to
ensure that the company will meet or exceed market expectations.

The best companies identify *leading indicators of value*—current
measures that strongly correlate with the business's long-term value
(chapter 6). Examples include time to market for new products,

employee turnover, customer retention rates, number of new stores opened on time, and the average cycle time from order date to shipping date. Frontline managers can influence all these operating initiatives. Improving leading-indicator performance is the foundation for achieving superior shareholder value added. Superior shareholder value added, in turn, is the foundation for superior shareholder returns. Figure 12-1 depicts this three-level hierarchy of performance measurement. Astute expectations investors always check to see how well a company aligns its incentive pay practices with shareholders' superior-return objective.

Expectations investors must understand incentive compensation to gauge the probability that a company will deliver results different from what the market expects. Companies that embrace compensation programs with superior performance standards send a powerful message to investors about their aspirations and are more likely to be the subject of positive revisions. Negative revisions are more likely for companies that pay for mediocrity through weak, equity-linked compensation programs.

FIGURE 12-1   The Hierarchy of Performance Measurement

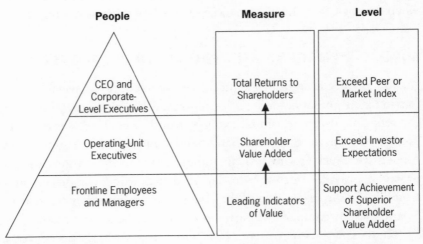

ESSENTIAL IDEAS

- Understanding executive and employee incentive compensation programs is essential to anticipating changes in market expectations.

- Standard executive stock options depart from the pay-for-superior-performance ideal because they reward any increase in share price—even when a company lags its competitors or the overall market.

- Indexed options appropriately reward executives for superior performance in bull and bear markets alike.

- Appropriate pay plans reward operating-unit executives for delivering superior shareholder value added, that is, value above market expectations.

notes

1 The Case for Expectations Investing

1. Louis E. Boone, *Quotable Business* (New York: Random House, 1999).
2. We assume that investors have already chosen investment policies that reflect their risk tolerance—the level of equity exposure and the degree of diversification in the equity sector.
3. Charles D. Ellis, *Winning the Loser's Game*, 3rd ed. (New York: McGraw Hill, 1998), 5.
4. "Where, Oh Where Are the .400 Hitters of Yesteryear?" *Financial Analysts Journal* 54, no. 6 (November–December 1998): 6–14.
5. John C. Bogle, *Common Sense on Mutual Funds: New Imperatives for the Intelligent Investor* (New York: John Wiley & Sons, 1999), 92.
6. Yet another cost is less obvious. As the size of their fund increases, portfolio managers incur market-impact costs. Market impact is the difference between an execution price and the posted price for a stock. For large-volume purchases or sales, the market impact may make the transaction not economically feasible. Therefore, a manager may have to hold stocks he or she no longer wants, which prevents the manager from buying stocks he or she does want to own. For further discussion, see Ben Warwick, *Searching for Alpha* (New York: John Wiley & Sons, 2000), 36–38.
7. Berkshire Hathaway Annual Report, 2000, 13.
8. Jack L. Treynor, "Long-Term Investing," *Financial Analysts Journal* 32, no. 3 (May–June 1976): 56.
9. John Burr Williams, *The Theory of Investment Value* (Cambridge: Harvard University Press, 1938), 186–191.
10. Research studies confirm that announced changes in accounting methods that alter reported earnings, but not cash flows, don't affect the stock price.

11. Jonathan Clements, "Vanguard Founder Blasts Funds' Focus," *Wall Street Journal*, 16 May 2000.
12. Alfred Rappaport, "CFOs and Strategists: Forging a Common Framework," *Harvard Business Review*, May–June 1992, 87.
13. Michael J. Mauboussin, Alexander Schay, and Stephen Kawaja, "Counting What Counts," *Credit Suisse First Boston Equity Research*, 2 February 2000.
14. Erick Schonfeld, "The Guidance Game," *Fortune*, 21 December 1998, 255.
15. To further complicate matters, the rules of the game have changed for companies that perennially beat consensus expectations. These companies have to meet an even higher standard—meeting so-called whisper numbers, that is, higher-than-consensus earnings expectations. These numbers are unofficial, but often prove to be closer to reported results than the "official" consensus estimates. Companies that top consensus estimates but fall short of whisper numbers often see their shares fall as investors trim expectations.
16. Price-earnings multiples are generally based on the next year's earnings-per-share estimate.

2 How the Market Values Stocks

1. Suppose someone offers you a contract specifying that you will receive $10,000 one year from today. What is the most you should pay for this contract today? The answer, of course, depends on the rate of return that you can expect to earn over the next year. If the one-year interest rate for investments of comparable risk is 7 percent, then you shouldn't pay more than the dollar amount, which, when compounded at a 7 percent rate, equals $10,000 by the end of the year. Since you know next year's cash flow ($10,000) and the discount rate (7 percent), you can easily determine that the present value, or the maximum that you should pay, is $9,346:

Present value × (1 + Rate of return) = Future value
Present value × 1.07 = $10,000
Present value = $9,346

2. Neil Barsky, "Empire Building to be Sold to a Peter Grace Family Member," *New York Times*, 31 October 1991.
3. John C. Bogle, "Investing Wisely in an Era of Greed," *Fortune*, 2 October 2000, 130.
4. You can generally estimate the adjustment between book and cash taxes by looking at the change in accumulated deferred taxes on the balance sheet (the net of deferred tax assets and deferred tax liabilities).
5. We deduct depreciation because it reasonably approximates the required spending to maintain current productive capacity. As a result, we consider

only capital investment above and beyond depreciation as an "incremental" investment. Note that we did not adjust operating profit to reflect depreciation expense—a noncash item. However, since we deduct depreciation from capital expenditures, free cash flow is truly a "cash" number. We could generate the identical free cash-flow number by adding depreciation back to operating profit and deducting total capital expenditures instead of incremental investment.

6. For example, liquidation value would be the best estimate of residual value for declining companies that are unlikely to sustain as going concerns.

7. Here's why. Suppose that shareholders invested $50 million of initial capital in a company five years ago. Over the next five years, the book value grew from the initial investment of $50 million to $70 million. Market value, however, increased to $100 million over the same period. Assume that a reasonable return is 11 percent. Are shareholders satisfied with an 11 percent return on the $70 million book value, or do they expect to earn 11 percent on the $100 million market value? Clearly, investors want a return on current market value.

8. We base our cost-of-equity calculations on the capital asset pricing model (CAPM). Despite repeated questioning of CAPM's validity for twenty years, it remains the most widely used model to quantify the relationship between risk and return. More important, no better alternative is currently available. Critics offer evidence that other factors beyond beta, such as company size and market-to-book value, contribute to variations in long-term stock returns. Yet no theory can explain these results. Although some academic researchers have correlated such factors with excess returns, we cannot be sure that, once discovered, these factors will yield excess returns in the future. So while we acknowledge the lively debate surrounding CAPM, we do not consider it central to the expectations investing approach.

9. By investing in a portfolio broadly representative of the overall equity market, you can "diversify away" substantially all the unsystematic risk—that is, risk specific to individual companies, such as the unexpected death of a CEO, or a fire that destroys a major production facility. Therefore, the market prices securities at levels that reward investors only for the nondiversifiable market risk—that is, the systematic risk in movements in the overall market. Beta is a measure of systematic risk.

10. For a detailed discussion of dividend models and expected returns, see Bradford Cornell, *The Equity Risk Premium* (New York: John Wiley & Sons, 1999), chapter 3.

11. Joseph Weber, "What to Do with All That %#* Cash," *Business Week*, 20 November 2000, 160.

12. For a discussion of cash management, see S. L. Mintz, "Lean Green Machines," *CFO Magazine*, July 2000, 79–94.

13. When valuing bonds or preferred stock, use market value rather than book value. Changing interest rates after issuance cause market values to diverge from book values. If, for example, interest rates rise, then market value will fall below book value. If you use book value, then you will overstate the present values of bonds and preferred stocks and therefore understate shareholder value. When interest rates decline, the reverse is true. You can find current prices for publicly traded bonds and preferred stock in newspapers (*Wall Street Journal* or *Investor's Business Daily*) or on financial Web sites such as Bloomberg.com. To estimate the value of debt that does not trade publicly, discount the interest payments at the current market rate for debt of comparable risk.

14. Pension assets and liabilities do not appear on the sponsoring company's balance sheet, but you can find them in footnote disclosures on the financial statements. This is the best place to find the funding status of a company's pension plans.

15. Calculate residual value by the perpetuity-with-inflation method (see equation 2-7 in the appendix) with an expected inflation rate of 2 percent:

$$
\begin{aligned}
\text{Residual value} &= \frac{(\text{NOPAT}) (1 + \text{Inflation rate})}{(\text{Cost of capital} - \text{Inflation rate})} \\
&= \frac{(\$11.455 \text{ million}) (1.02)}{(0.10 - 0.02)} \\
&= \$146.05 \text{ million}
\end{aligned}
$$

Discounting the above residual value at the 10 percent cost-of-capital rate over the five-year period yields $90.69 million.

16. The perpetuity assumption is much less aggressive than it might initially appear, because as cash flows become more distant, their value in present-value terms becomes correspondingly smaller. For example, a $1.00 perpetuity discounted at 15 percent has a value of $1.00 divided by 15 percent, or $6.67. Here are the present values for annual annuities of $1.00 for periods ranging from five to twenty-five years:

Years	Present Value of Annuity	Percentage of Perpetuity Value
5	$3.35	50.2%
10	5.02	75.3
15	5.85	87.7
20	6.26	93.9
25	6.46	96.9

Note that by year 10, we reach 75 percent of the perpetuity value and by year 15, it approaches 90 percent. As the discount rate increases, the time to reach perpetuity value decreases.

17. If we were to revise the discount rate in the perpetuity model from nominal to real terms, the valuation would equal the valuation that the perpetuity-with-inflation model generates. For example, assume a real cost of capital of 7.84 percent, and expected inflation of 2 percent. The nominal cost of capital is [(1 + real cost of capital) × (1 + expected inflation)] − 1. In this example, the nominal cost of capital is [(1 + 0.0784) (1 + 0.02)] − 1, or 10 percent. Now assume that free cash flow before new investment for the last year of the forecast period is $1.00. Residual value with the perpetuity method is $1.00 divided by 10 percent, or $10.00. Converting the perpetuity model from nominal to real terms, we divide the $1.00 by the real cost of capital of 7.84 percent to obtain $12.75 for residual value—the same value that the perpetuity-with-inflation model generates.

3 The Expectations Infrastructure

1. Peter Coy, "The Power of Smart Pricing," *Business Week*, 10 April 2000, 160.
2. Adrian Slywotzky and Joao Baptista, "AT&T Finds Bigger Isn't Always Better," *Wall Street Journal*, 27 October 2000.
3. Michael E. Porter, *Competitive Advantage: Creating and Sustaining Superior Performance* (New York: Free Press, 1985), 73.
4. David Besanko pointed out to us that economies of scale also might affect investments. For example, as volume grows over time, a manufacturing company may be able to invest in larger, more automated plants that reduce its incremental investment rate. We believe that economies of scale for investment are extraordinarily difficult to assess and rarely significant in expectations investing. Consequently, we do not incorporate them in the expectations infrastructure.
5. David Besanko, David Dranove, and Mark Shanley, *Economics of Strategy* (New York: John Wiley & Sons, 2000), 436.
6. General Electric Annual Report, 1999, 5.
7. For a detailed look at how companies can sensibly reduce their capital expenditures, see Tom Copeland, "Cutting Costs Without Drawing Blood," *Harvard Business Review*, September–October 2000, 155. According to Copeland's research, a permanent 15 percent cut in capital spending could increase the market capitalization of some companies by as much as 30 percent.
8. Emily Nelson, "Wal-Mart Sets Supply Plan as Net Tops Forecasts," *Wall Street Journal*, 10 November 1999.
9. In this case, we hold the required incremental investment constant.
10. The term *threshold margin* first appeared in Alfred Rappaport, "Selecting Strategies That Create Shareholder Value," *Harvard Business Review*, May–June 1981, 139–149.

11. The formula for threshold margin, using perpetuity with inflation for residual value, is as follows:

$$\text{Threshold margin}_t = \frac{(\text{Operating profit margin}_{t-1})\,(1 + \text{Inflation rate})}{(1 + \text{Sales growth rate}_t)} +$$

$$\frac{[(\text{Sales growth rate}_t)/(1 + \text{Sales growth rate}_t)]\,(\text{Incremental investment rate})\,(\text{Cost of capital} - \text{Inflation rate})}{(1 - \text{Cash tax rate})\,(1 + \text{Cost of capital})}$$

where t equals the specified forecast year.

4 Analyzing Competitive Strategy

1. Michael E. Porter, *Competitive Strategy: Techniques for Analyzing Industries and Competitors* (New York: Free Press, 1980).
2. Michael E. Porter, *Competitive Advantage: Creating and Sustaining Superior Performance* (New York: Free Press, 1985), 36.
3. Adrian J. Slywotzky, *Value Migration: How to Think Several Moves Ahead of the Competition* (Boston: Harvard Business School Press, 1996); Adrian J. Slywotzky and David J. Morrison, *The Profit Zone: How Strategic Business Design Will Lead You to Tomorrow's Profits* (New York: Times Business, 1997).
4. Clayton M. Christensen and Matt Verlinden, "Disruption, Disintegration, and the Dissipation of Differentiability," working paper, Harvard Business School, Boston, January 2000.
5. Philip Evans and Thomas S. Wurster, *Blown to Bits: How the New Economics of Information Transforms Strategy* (Boston: Harvard Business School Press, 2000).
6. Adrian J. Slywotzky et al., *Profit Patterns: Thirty Ways to Anticipate and Profit from Strategic Forces Reshaping Your Business* (New York: Times Books, 1999), 123.
7. Evans and Wurster, *Blown to Bits*, 39–43.
8. Clayton M. Christensen, *The Innovator's Dilemma: When New Technologies Cause Great Firms to Fail* (Boston: Harvard Business School Press, 1997).
9. Ibid., 32.
10. Andrew S. Grove, *Only the Paranoid Survive* (New York: Currency/Doubleday, 1996).
11. Clayton M. Christensen and Richard S. Tedlow, "Patterns of Disruption in Retailing," *Harvard Business Review*, January–February 2000, 42–45.
12. Michael Schrage, "Getting Beyond the Innovation Fetish," *Fortune*, 13 November 2000, 225–232.
13. Carl Shapiro and Hal R. Varian, *Information Rules: A Strategic Guide to the Network Economy* (Boston: Harvard Business School Press, 1999).

14. W. Brian Arthur, "Increasing Returns and the New World of Business," *Harvard Business Review*, July–August 1996, 101–109.

15. Shapiro and Varian, *Information Rules*, 117.

5 How to Estimate Price-Implied Expectations

1. Warren E. Buffett, "How Inflation Swindles the Equity Investor," *Fortune*, 5 May 1977, 250.

2. Chris Kenney, "Market Signals Analysis: A Vital Tool for Managing Market Expectations," *L.E.K. Shareholder Value Added Newsletter*, vol. 9, p. 4.

3. Aswath Damodaran, "Homepage," *http://www.stern.nyu.edu/~adamodar*, offers a full cost-of-capital discussion and many complementary tools.

4. The market-implied forecast period was introduced under the name "value growth duration" in Alfred Rappaport, *Creating Shareholder Value: The New Standard for Business Performance* (New York: Free Press, 1986). For a detailed discussion of the role of the market-implied forecast period in security analysis, see Michael Mauboussin and Paul Johnson, "Competitive Advantage Period: The Neglected Value Driver," *Financial Management* 26, no. 2 (Summer 1997): 67–74. The authors call the forecast period the "competitive advantage period."

5. In a vast majority of cases, as long as the number and exercise price of options are fixed in advance, their cost never hits the income statement. However, the cost of options *is* reflected on the income statement under two conditions. The first is if a company chooses a program with a variable-option strike price. For example, a company can tie the changes in its option strike price to an index. In this case, the company records annual changes in the option's intrinsic value (stock price minus exercise price plus time value) on its income statement. The second is when a company "reprices" its options, or lowers the strike price. Repricings trigger a change in treatment from a "fixed" to a "variable" program, which affects the income statement. For more on indexed options, see Alfred Rappaport, "New Thinking on How to Link Executive Pay with Performance," *Harvard Business Review*, March–April 1999, 91–101.

6. Brian J. Hall, "What You Need to Know About Stock Options," *Harvard Business Review*, March–April 2000, 123.

7. It is important to distinguish between the cost borne by shareholders and the value of option grants to executives. Risk-averse, undiversified executives typically attach a lower value to their option grants.

8. For an excellent reference for options pricing models, see John C. Hull, *Options, Futures, and Other Derivatives* (New York: Prentice Hall, 1999).

9. Brian J. Hall and Kevin J. Murphy, "Stock Options for Undiversified Executives," working paper, October 2000; Nalin Kulatilaka and Alan J. Marcus, "Valuing Employee Stock Options," *Financial Analysts Journal* 50 (November–December 1994): 46–56; Jennifer N. Carpenter, "The Exercise and Valuation of Executive Stock Options," *Journal of Financial Economics* 48 (1998): 127–158; and Lisa Meulbrook, "The Efficiency of Equity-Linked Compensation: Understanding the Full Cost of Awarding Executive Stock Options," working paper, Harvard Business School, Boston, 2000.

10. In the company's 2000 annual report, Microsoft states that options "generally vest over four and one-half years . . . while certain options vest . . . over seven and one-half years" (Microsoft Annual Report, 2000), 29. We have assumed five years as an average.

11. Technically, employee stock options are not options—they're warrants. A financial option is the right but not the obligation to buy or sell a share that is already outstanding. A warrant is the right to purchase a new share at a specified price. Because warrants are dilutive, they are slightly less valuable than options. The warrant conversion factor is $1/[1 + (\text{number of ESOs/number of shares})]$. The warrant conversion factor turns out to be 97.2 percent, and therefore reduces the value by less than 3 percent.

12. More accurately, this consideration applies for nonqualified option grants. Qualified options, on the other hand, provide no tax deduction for the corporation. Nonqualified programs constitute a large majority of all option grants, but some start-ups do grant a substantial number of qualified options.

6 Identifying Expectations Opportunities

1. Thomas H. Nodine, "Home Depot's Leading Indicators of Value," sidebar in Rappaport, "Executive Pay," *Harvard Business Review*, March–April 1999, 100.

2. J. Edward Russo and Paul J. H. Schoemaker, "Managing Overconfidence," *Sloan Management Review* 33, no. 2 (Winter 1992): 7–17.

3. Hersh Shefrin, *Beyond Greed and Fear: Understanding Behavioral Finance and the Psychology of Investing* (Boston: Harvard Business School Press, 2000), 20.

4. Anne K. Bui et al., "Worldwide PC Forecast Update, 1999–2003," *IDC Bulletin #W20599* (November 1999).

5. David Bovet and Joseph Martha, *Value Nets: Breaking the Supply Chain to Unlock Hidden Profits* (New York: John Wiley & Sons, 2000), 139–155.

6. Gary D. Goodman, "Gateway, Inc.," *Value Line Investment Survey*, 21 April 2000, 1104. The high-end estimate assumes that Gateway can sus-

tain this sales growth rate for the full seven-year market-implied forecast period.

7. Based on a conversation with Charles R. Wolf, PC analyst at Needham & Co.

8. Jim Davis and Michael Kanellos, "AOL, Gateway in Far-Reaching Pact," CNET News.com, 20 October 1999, *http://news.cnet.com/news/0-1006-200-920643.html* (accessed April 2001).

7 Buy, Sell, or Hold?

1. Max H. Bazerman, *Judgment in Managerial Decision Making* (New York: John Wiley & Sons, 1998), 6–8, 39–41.

2. We use the term *excess return* to depict better-than-cost-of-capital returns for an individual stock. We use the term *superior returns* throughout the book to mean performance above an appropriate benchmark for an investor's entire stock portfolio.

3. Assume a $100 expected value, a current stock price of $80 (80 percent of expected value), and a 10 percent cost of capital. We obtain the expected value two years from now, $121, by taking today's $100 expected value and compounding it at the 10 percent cost of capital rate. If the $80 stock price rises to $121 at the end of the two years, the annual return is 22.9 percent. Subtracting the cost of capital gives an excess return of 12.9 percent, or about 13 percent.

4. Richard H. Thaler, "Saving, Fungibility, and Mental Accounts," *Journal of Economic Perspectives* 4, no. 1 (1990): 193–205.

5. Shefrin, *Beyond Greed and Fear*, 214–218.

6. Daniel Kahneman and Amos Tversky, "Prospect Theory: An Analysis of Decision Under Risk," *Econometrica* 47, no. 2 (1979): 263–291.

7. Terrance Odean, "Are Investors Reluctant to Realize Their Losses?" *Journal of Finance* 53 (October 1998): 1775–1798.

8. This analysis applies to taxable investment accounts and not to tax-deferred accounts such as 401(k)s.

9. Brad Barber and Terrance Odean, "Trading Is Hazardous to Your Wealth: The Common Stock Investment Performance of Individual Investors," *Journal of Finance* 55, no. 2 (2000): 773–806.

8 Beyond Discounted Cash Flow

1. We are indebted to Martha Amram for helping us to develop these techniques.

2. Readers who want to learn more about how to identify and value real options should consult Martha Amram and Nalin Kulatilaka, *Real Options*

(Boston: Harvard Business School Press, 1999). Also, see their Web site, *www.real-options.com*.

3. Nalin Kulatilaka and Alan J. Marcus, "Project Valuation under Uncertainty: When Does DCF Fail?" *Journal of Applied Corporate Finance* 5, no. 3 (Fall 1992): 92–100; and Amram and Kulatilaka, *Real Options*.

4. The option to abandon is analogous to a put option.

5. Dividend payments also affect option value. We set aside dividends to simplify this example.

6. Richard A. Brealey and Stewart C. Myers, *Principles of Corporate Finance*, 5th ed. (New York: Irwin McGraw Hill, 1996), appendix 12–13.

7. A European call option assumes that the exercise decision occurs only at option expiration. American options assume that the exercise decision can come at any time during the option's life. Given that there are no dividend payments, the European and American call values are identical in this case.

8. Net present value = $S - X = 0$ means that $S = X$. Accordingly, $S/X = 1$.

9. Steven R. Grenadier, "Option Exercise Games: The Intersection of Real Options and Game Theory," *Journal of Applied Corporate Finance* 13, no. 2 (Summer 2000): 99–107.

10. It is important to consider these past investments, especially when a company is investing in mergers and acquisitions or joint ventures. One spectacular example is when Cisco Systems acquired Cerent Corporation for $6.9 billion in November 1999. In the first half of 1999, Cerent's sales were less than $10 million. We probably cannot justify Cerent on a value-added basis, but the deal most likely created substantial real-options value for Cisco. Because of Cisco's prior investments in infrastructure, it could grow Cerent's business much faster and more cost effectively than any other competitor. Indeed, the market agreed. The day that the deal was announced, Cisco's stock rose.

11. Look at the price of the option and the other four inputs. Use the valuation formula to solve for the level of implied volatility consistent with the trading price of the option. See Amram and Kulatilaka, *Real Options*; or Hull, *Options, Futures, and Other Derivatives*, for how to estimate volatility. See also *www.ivolatility.com* for current volatility estimates using these two methods.

12. This is the case for reinventors such as Enron. Here we might use an average volatility estimated from the new business. Enron's original business, gas pipelines, has a considerably lower volatility than its new businesses, quasi-investment banking in key commodity markets.

13. Martha Amram and Nalin Kulatilaka, "Strategy and Shareholder Value Creation: The Real Options Frontier," *Journal of Applied Corporate Finance* 13, no. 2 (Summer 2000): 15–28.

14. Since the *magnitude* of expected-value creation for the established businesses isn't large enough to reach the stock price, the model must artificially extend the *duration* of value creation to compensate.

15. Alfred Rappaport, "Tips for Investing in Internet Stocks," *Wall Street Journal*, 24 February 2000.

16. Note that the lower stock price also substantially reduces the ESO liability. In this case, the ESO liability was roughly cut in half, exclusive of any new grants. This underscores the notion that the ESO liability is dynamic.

17. Company managers can help this process by telling a great story. See J. William Gurley, "The Great Art of Storytelling," *Fortune*, 8 November 1999.

18. George Soros, *The Alchemy of Finance: Reading the Mind of the Market* (New York: John Wiley & Sons, 1994), 49.

19. In a secondary offering, public investors supply financing as a company sells new shares. In a stock-financed acquisition, the shareholders of the selling company supply the financing.

9 Across the Economic Landscape

1. David Sheff, "Crank It Up," *Wired*, August 2000, 186–197.

2. Brent Schlender, "The Bill and Warren Show," *Fortune*, 20 July 1998, 48–64.

3. Paul M. Romer, "Endogenous Technological Change," *Journal of Political Economy* 98, no. 5 (1990): S71–S102.

4. Shapiro and Varian, *Information Rules*, 179.

5. Employee stock options, a significant form of remuneration for many knowledge companies, is not expensed.

6. The *tipping point* is an important related idea. The term refers to the level of market share at which future market-share gains become cheaper and cheaper to acquire, leading a single firm or technology to overcome all others. For a given product, the tipping point is equivalent to reaching critical mass—market-share momentum that assures incremental success. A market is likely to tip if two factors are in place: low demand for variety and high economies of scale. Low demand for variety means that the market accepts either a formal or a de facto standard. Digital videodiscs (DVDs) and Microsoft PC operating systems are examples of useful standardization. In contrast, standardization in another knowledge industry—the drug industry—doesn't make much sense. Consumers need a variety of solutions for their health-care needs.

7. Investors must first identify the sectors in which the network effects are intense. Strong network effects tend to occur when the network participants enjoy a high degree of interactivity and compatibility. Next,

investors must find the companies most likely to translate the benefits of network effects into shareholder value.

8. For a detailed discussion of this, see Geoffrey A. Moore, *Crossing the Chasm: Marketing and Selling High-Tech Products to Mainstream Customers* (New York: HarperBusiness, 1991); Geoffrey A. Moore, *Inside the Tornado: Marketing Strategies from Silicon Valley's Cutting Edge* (New York: HarperBusiness, 1995); Geoffrey A. Moore, Paul Johnson, and Tom Kippola, *Gorilla Game: An Investor's Guide to Picking Winners in High Technology* (New York: HarperBusiness, 1998).

9. Christensen, *The Innovator's Dilemma*, 88.

10. Robert Guy Matthews, "The Outlook," *Wall Street Journal*, 23 October 2000.

11. Replication and distribution are not necessarily *both* inexpensive. For example, replication of a music CD may be cheap, but distribution through a traditional store format remains costly.

12. At any point in a drug's development, a company can choose to abandon research and development.

13. Sibylle Hechtel, "Biotech's Burn Rate," *Red Herring*, April 2000, 322–323.

14. Federal Reserve Bank of Dallas Annual Report, 1999, 20.

15. The Home Depot Annual Report, 1999, 19.

16. David Besanko, David Dranove, and Mark Shanley, *Economics of Strategy* (New York: John Wiley & Sons, 2000), 92.

17. Ibid., 86–87.

18. 8-K, September 15, 1997, 1–2.

19. Recall that most investments by service and knowledge businesses are expensed and that efficiencies related to these investments are therefore considered cost efficiencies.

20. David Blanchard, "Flow Manufacturing Pulls Through," *Evolving Enterprise* 2, no. 1 (February/March 1999).

21. General Electric Annual Report, 1994, 2.

22. James F. Clark, "1999 Integrated Oils Financial Almanac," *Credit Suisse First Boston Equity Research*, 27 May 1999.

23. Copeland, "Cutting Costs Without Drawing Blood," 155–164.

10 Mergers and Acquisitions

1. Sometimes an acquisition represents part of a more global, long-term strategy to attain a competitive advantage. What is important is that the *overall* strategy adds a satisfactory level of value. In such a situation, the acquiring company may not expect a particular purchase to contribute value, but purchasing may be the only feasible way to execute the strategy. Such an acquisition does not represent an end in itself; rather, it provides the real option to participate in future value-generating opportunities.

Expectations investors should, however, be wary of CEOs who use real-options rhetoric to rationalize poorly conceived acquisitions or overpayments. For a comprehensive treatment of the difficulty of producing synergies, see Mark L. Sirower, *The Synergy Trap* (New York: Free Press, 1997).

2. When the seller is publicly traded, market value is the best basis for establishing stand-alone value. For some companies—specifically, those whose stocks have been bid up in anticipation of a takeover—market value may not be a particularly good proxy for stand-alone value. To estimate stand-alone value, deduct the "takeover premium" impounded in the current market price from the current market price.

3. A quick litmus test is to capitalize management's after-tax synergy forecast by the cost of capital and compare it to the premium. For example, with an expected $100 million in pretax savings, a 35 percent tax rate, and a 10 percent cost of capital, capitalized after-tax synergies are worth $100 million × (1 − 35%)/10% = $650 million.

4. This section and the next are adapted from Alfred Rappaport and Mark L. Sirower, "Stock or Cash? The Trade-Offs for Buyers and Sellers in Mergers and Acquisitions," *Harvard Business Review*, November–December 1999, 147–158.

5. Ibid., 156–158.

6. Although the market's short-term response to a merger announcement provides a reasonably reliable barometer of the likely consequences of the transaction, with hindsight the market assessment might just turn out to be incorrect. Research has shown, however, that the market's assessments are unbiased—which means that, on average, the market neither overvalues nor undervalues the transaction. There is an approximately fifty-fifty probability that the market assessment will be either too low or too high in estimating the eventual value created by the merger. We can view investors' collective judgment as an objective assessment of the merger's value to buying and selling shareholders. In brief, the immediate price reaction is the market's best estimate of the long-term implications of the transaction. For those who believe that the market erred in its response to a merger announcement, an opportunity exists to profitably buy or sell shares.

11 Share Buybacks

1. Companies finance these programs through internally generated cash flow, cash on the balance sheet, or issuance of debt.

2. As Warren Buffett said in Berkshire Hathaway's 1984 annual report, "When companies with outstanding businesses and comfortable financial positions find their shares selling far below intrinsic value in the market-

place, no alternative action can benefit shareholders as surely as repurchases" (Berkshire Hathaway Inc., "Letters to Shareholders 1977–1986," 85).

3. Michael C. Jensen, "Corporate Control and the Politics of Finance," *Journal of Applied Corporate Finance* 4, no. 2 (Summer 1991): 13–33.

4. Companies and investors often incorrectly associate the "return" from a buyback with accounting-based measures, like the inverse of the P/E multiple. The (faulty) logic is as follows: Say the consensus expects a company to earn $1 per share. The shares trade at $25, a P/E ratio of 25. So the company gets $1 in earnings for every $25 share it buys back, a "return" of 4 percent (1/25). The flaw in this analysis is that investors cannot reliably link a P/E multiple to the cost of equity, because multiples are a shorthand that incorporate variables other than the discount rate. These variables include growth, operating margins, investment needs, and the sustainability of competitive advantage.

5. Rappaport, *Creating Shareholder Value*, 96.

6. Reinvestment opportunities range from relatively high returns to returns modestly above the cost of capital. Naturally, management should target lower-return opportunities for further scrutiny. However, some low-return investments, such as those for environmental controls, may be regulated, and therefore, investors cannot avoid them. Other investments appear to generate low returns until you consider the consequences of *not* investing. Yet other investments may not fully incorporate the benefits to other products or services in rate-of-return calculations.

7. A month before the market crash in October 1987, Louis Harris and Associates polled 1,000 CEOs. The pollsters asked, "Is the current price of your stock an accurate indicator of its real value?" Of the 58 percent who responded no, virtually all believed that the market was undervaluing their shares.

8. Clifford Stephens and Michael Weisbach, "Actual Share Reacquisitions in Open-Market Repurchase Programs," *Journal of Finance* 53, no. 1 (1998): 313–333.

9. William McNally, "Who Wins in Large Stock Buybacks—Those Who Sell or Those Who Hold?" *Journal of Applied Corporate Finance* 11, no. 1 (Spring 1998): 78–88. McNally shows that the nontendering shareholders who "pay" the tendering shareholders for the premium through a wealth transfer are rewarded by the market's positive reaction to management's positive signal.

10. Ranjan D'Emello and Pervin K. Shroff, "Equity Undervaluation and Decisions Related to Repurchase Tender Offers: An Empirical Investigation," *Journal of Finance* 55 (October 2000): 2399–2324.

11. Theo Vermaelen, "Common Stock Repurchases and Market Signaling," *Journal of Financial Economics* 9 (1981): 139–183.

12. A Microsoft press release articulates this point: "The number of shares to be purchased during fiscal 2001 will be based on several factors, primarily

the level of employee stock option exercises" ("Microsoft Announces Share Repurchase Program," press release, 7 August 2000). *http://www. microsoft.com/presspass/press/2000/Aug00/BuybackInitiationPR.asp.*

13. Robert O'Brien, "Deals and Deal Makers: Stock Buybacks Gain Popularity, but Price Pops Aren't Guaranteed," *Wall Street Journal*, 6 March 2000.

14. The results are the same if we assume that the companies borrowed to fund the program instead.

15. Eugene F. Fama and Kenneth R. French, "Disappearing Dividends: Changing Firm Characteristics or Lower Propensity to Pay?" working paper 509, Center for Research in Security Prices, June 2000.

16. Our statements relate to the United States. Other countries have different tax rates and policies.

17. All shareholders on record date are eligible to receive a dividend. The *ex-dividend* day is the first day of trading when the seller, rather than the buyer, of a stock will be entitled to the most recently announced dividend payment. This date is currently two business days before the record date. A stock that has gone ex-dividend generally trades lower by the amount of the dividend. So when a $100 stock pledging a $1 dividend goes ex-dividend, the trading price drops to $99.

18. For a more sophisticated approach, see John R. Graham, "How Big Are the Tax Benefits of Debt?" *Journal of Finance* 55 (October 2000): 1901–1941.

12 Incentive Compensation

1. This chapter is adapted from Rappaport, "Executive Pay," 91–101.

2. The exercise price for conventional stock options is the price on the day that the options are granted. It stays fixed over the entire option period, usually ten years. If the share price exceeds the exercise price, then the option holder can cash in on the gains.

3. Hall, "What You Need to Know," 121–129.

4. For example, a 20 percent increase on a $100 stock is worth more than the same 20 percent increase on a lower-priced stock.

5. For a detailed presentation of the incentive implications of indexed options, see Shane A. Johnson and Yisong S. Tian, "Indexed Executive Stock Options," *Journal of Financial Economics* 57, no. 1 (2000): 35–64.

6. Level 3 Communications Inc., an operator of fiber-optic phone networks, is the commonly cited exception.

7. For a detailed explanation of the differences between shareholder value added and residual income, see Rappaport, *Creating Shareholder Value*, 119–128.

8. For a detailed explanation of how to estimate superior shareholder value added, see Rappaport, "Executive Pay," 97–99.

index

abandonment option, 119
accounting
    business categories and, 139–140
    earnings determinations and,
      11–12
    ESOs and, 78
    indexed options and, 190
    mental, 112
accounting-based tools, 5
accounts payable, 26
active management, 4–7
    costs of, 5
    incentives in, 5–6
    investing styles and, 6–7
    tools for, 5
Adams, Kirby, 143
adaptation, 65
Amazon.com, 62, 118
    real options value at, 128–132
American Standard, 147–148
America Online, 102–103
anchoring, 91
Andreessen, Marc, 137
Arthur, W. Brian, 65
assets
    nonoperating, 34, 72
    in the value chain, 60

Baptista, Joao, 44
Barber, Brad, 115
Barnes & Noble, 62
barriers to entry, 55, 93
benchmarks
    expectations, 1–2
    underperformance of by
      institutional investors, 4–7
    volatility, 124–125
Bernstein, Peter L., 4, xi–xiv
beta coefficient, 31, 72
Bezos, Jeff, 129
bias, in probabilities, 106–107
Black-Scholes formula, 121, 122
Bogle, John, 5, 9–10, 20
bonds, 20
Borders, 62
Buffett, Warren, 6, 70, 112
businesses, categories of, 135–149
    characteristics of, 136–140
    value factors and, 140–149
business models, 139
buy, sell, hold decisions, 8, 105–116
    choosing buy, 110–112
    choosing sell, 112–114
    expected-value analysis for,
      105–108

buy, sell, hold decisions (*continued*)
Gateway case study for, 108–110
taxes and, 114–115
buybacks. *See* share buybacks
buyer power, 56, 93

capacity
competitor moves and adding, 57
as investment trigger, 137
capital
changes in working, 25–26
investments in working and fixed,
11, 25–27
structure of, 173
time value of, 11
capitalism, xi–xiv
Capital (Marx), xi–xii
cash, excess, 33–34
cash conversion cycles, 46, 97
cash flow
determining, 21, 23
free, 22–28
sources for, 71–72
as stock price basis, 19–21
cash offers, 162, 163–164, 166–167
cash tax rate, as value determinant,
22–23
Charles Schwab & Co., 59
Christensen, Clay, 59, 61
Clark, James, 148
compensation, incentive, 185–195
competitive advantage period, 73
competitive strategy analysis,
51–66
disruptive technology framework
for, 61–63
finding expectations opportunities
with, 86–90
five forces framework for, 54–57
frameworks for, 53–65

historical analysis, 52–53
information rules framework for,
63–65
uses of, 51–52
value chain framework for, 58–60
competitors, anticipating moves of,
57
compounding, 19
confirmation trap, 114
consensus-tracking services, 71
Copeland, Tom, 148–149
core competencies, 60
corporate value
determining, 21
versus shareholder value, 33–34
cost efficiencies, 89
business categories and, 145–147
as value factor, 44–45
cost of capital, 11, 28–32, 72, 88
opportunities and, 88
weighting, 28–29
costs
as turbo trigger, 87–89
up-front versus incremental, 63
customers
locking in, 64
needs of, 62
priorities of, 59

debt
average, by industry, 28–29
in expectations analysis, 72
share buybacks and, 182–183
shareholder value and, 34
deconstruction, value chain, 60
Dell Computer, 45, 92
demand-flow technology, 147–148
discounted cash-flow model, 2
equity, 32
estimating expectations with, 7

financial service companies and,
32
price setting by, 20
time value of money in, 11
Williams on, 8
discounting, 19
disruptive technology, 61–63, 95
distribution channels, 59, 94
dividends, 181–182
dividend yield, 79
drug development, 143
Dutch auctions, 176

earnings announcements, market
response to, 9
earnings per share (EPS), 154–155
buybacks to manage, 178–180
value growth versus, 15–16
value information of, 10–13
Eastman Kodak Company, 57,
148–149
eBay, 64, 141
economics, knowledge-based
companies and, 63
economies of scale
business categories and, 143–145
supply-side versus demand-side,
138–140
as value factor, 43–44
volume purchasing and, 143–144
economies of scope, 144–145
Electronic Data Systems
Corporation (EDS), 76
employees
attracting and retaining, 133
incentive compensation and,
185–195
employee stock options (ESOs),
78–84, 185–195
already-granted, 80–83

dividends and, 182
estimating, 72
factors affecting value of, 78–80
fixed-number plans, 188
fixed-value plans, 188
future, 83–84
indexed-option programs,
189–191
megagrants, 188–189
option cancellations, 82–83
repricing decision, 190–191
share buybacks and, 178–180
shareholder value and, 34
valuing, 78–84
Enron, 118
environment, 72
equity
average, by industry, 28–29
estimating cost of, 29–32
share buybacks and, 182–183
equity discounted cash-flow model,
32
equity financing, 132–133
equity risk premium, 30
escalation trap, 111–112
Evans, Philip, 60
executives, compensation for,
186–193
exercise price, 79
expansion option, 118–119
expectations
benchmarking, 1–2
estimating, 7, 69–84
managing, 13
mismatches, 85, 105
price-implied, 69–84
revising, 39–49
sales, 46–47
selecting appropriate, 1–2
structure of, 1–2
threshold margin and, 47–48

expectations (*continued*)
   time for market to revise, 111
expectations infrastructure, 39–49
expectations investing
   applicability of, 8
   process of, 7–8
   support for, 1–16
expected-value analysis, 105–108
   Gateway case study, 108–110
   updating, 109–110
extension option, 118–119

fair disclosure, 3
Fama, Eugene, 181–182
Financial Accounting Standards
      Board, 78
financial call options, 119–122
financial service companies, 32, 59
five forces framework, 54–57
fixed-price tender offers, 176–177
fixed-share offers, 160–161, 167
fixed-value offers, 161–162, 163,
      167–168
flexibility, 119
forecast period, 33
   market-implied, 33, 73, 74–76, 88
French, Kenneth, 181–182
Fuji, 57

game theory, 57
Gates, Bill, 137
Gateway
   business model, 92, 95
   cash flows, 73–74
   competitive analysis of, 92–95
   cost of capital, 74
   expectations opportunities and,
      92–104
   expected-value analysis of,
      108–110

historical analysis of, 95–104
market-implied forecast period,
      74–76
nonoperating assets and debt, 74
sales growth at, 101–103
General Electric, 45
giveaways, 64–65
Greenspan, Alan, 190
Gretzky, Wayne, 2
Grove, Andy, 62
growth investments, 6–7
growth strategy, 133–134

Hall, Brian, 188
historical data
   finding expectations opportunities
      with, 86–90
   on Gateway, 95–104
   investment rates, 25
   in strategy analysis, 52–53
   value driver performance, 72
hold decisions. *See* buy, sell, hold
      decisions
holding periods, 9–10
Holliday, Shaun, 133
Home Depot, The,
   earnings and cash flow for, 12
   economies of scale at, 144
   leading indicators for, 89–90
Hotmail, 64–65
house-money effect, 112

Ibbotson.com, 72
incentive compensation, 185–195
   threshold for, 192–193
incremental fixed capital investment
      rate, 25
incremental working capital
      investment rate, 25
industry attractiveness, 53–54

industry stability, 52–53, 124–125

industry structure, 53

inflation, perpetuity-with-inflation method and, 37–38

information
  anchoring, 91
  confirmation trap of, 114
  in the value chain, 60

information rules framework, 63–65

initial public offerings (IPOs), 182

insider selling, 177

interest rates, 88

Internet, financial services distribution via, 59

inventories, 26

investment efficiencies, 147–149
  as value factor, 45–46

investment misconceptions, 9–14

investments
  buybacks versus, 174–175
  at Gateway, 97
  as turbo trigger, 87–89
  as value driver, 22–23

Kahneman, Daniel, 113

Kellogg Company, 145, 146

knowledge businesses, 136. *See also* businesses, categories of
  characteristics of, 63–65
  demand in, 141–142
  first-to-scale advantages, 145

leading indicators of value, 89–90
  at Gateway, 101–103

learning curve, 144

L.E.K. Consulting, 71–72, 89, 187

liabilities. *See also* debt
  employee stock options, 34, 80–84
  working capital and, 26

life of option, 120

link-and-leverage, 65

Living.com, 133

lock-in, 64

loss-aversion phenomenon, 113–114

Loudcloud, 137

management
  active investment, 4–7
  assessing information from, 71
  merger/acquisition signals by, 162–164
  objectives of, 51
  overconfidence of, 175
  real-options analysis and, 125–126
  signals in share buybacks, 172–173
  synergy estimates of, 155–156

margin of safety, 8, 110–111

market, as short term versus long term, 9–10, 70

market-implied forecast period, 73
  finding opportunities and, 88
  Gateway's, 74–76

market-imputed real-options value, 126–127

market leaders, 61, 126

market risk premium, 30, 72

Marx, Karl, xi–xii

McDonald's, 45, 148

mental accounting, 112

mergers and acquisitions, 153–169
  acquiring company burden in, 158–159
  anticipating stock market reaction to, 164–168
  assessing impact of, 157–162
  cash offers, 166–167
  fixed-share offers, 167
  fixed-value offers, 167–168
  management signals in, 162–164
  significance of, 153
  stock price assessments in, 3

mergers and acquisitions (*continued*)
  synergy evaluation for, 155–156
  value added by, 154–155
Merrill Lynch, 59
Microsoft, 63
  ESO value at, 80–81, 82, 83, 84
mix
  business categories and, 141–142
  as value factor, 42
mutual funds
  costs of, 5
  incentives for managers of, 5–6
  investing styles of, 6–7
  versus private investing, 3
  tools used by, 5
  underperformance of benchmarks
    by, 4–7

Napster, 138
net operating profit after taxes
    (NOPAT)
  determining, 21, 25–26
  in perpetuity calculations, 36–37
  residual value and, 26–27
  sales growth and, 47
network effects, 63–64, 141–142
Nodine, Thomas H., 89
nonrival goods, 137–138
Novell, 146
Nucor, 44

obsolescence, 137
Odean, Terrance, 114, 115
offerings, 59, 94–95
open-market purchases, 176
operating leverage
  business categories and, 142–143
  compared to economies of scale,
    44

as transitory, 143
as value factor, 42–43
operating profit
  determining, 21
  at Gateway, 96–97
  margin as value driver, 22–23
  shareholder value and, 47–48
opportunities, identifying, 7–8,
    85–104
  Gateway case study, 92–104
  pitfalls in, 90–91
  searching for, 86–90
options, employee. *See* employee
    stock options (ESOs)
options, real. *See* real-options
    analysis
overconfidence, 90–91, 115
  of management, 175

payoffs, determining, 106
performance standards, incentive
    compensation and, 186–195
perpetuity method
  estimating residual value with,
    26–27
  for residual value calculations,
    36–37
perpetuity-with-inflation method
  estimating residual value with,
    26–27
  for residual values calculations,
    37–38
physical companies, 136
politician's-pledge problem,
    175–176
Porter, Michael, 54–55, 58
premium at risk, 160–162
preproduction costs, 42–43
  business categories and, 142–143
present value, 19–20

price
  business categories and, 141–142
  as value factor, 42
price-earnings (PE) multiples
  mergers/acquisitions and, 154–155
  value determination and, 13–14
price-implied expectations (PIE),
    70–84
  cash flows in, 71–72
  cost of capital in, 72
  employee stock options and,
    78–84
  finding expectations opportunities
    with, 86–90
  at Gateway, 97–98
  Gateway case study of, 73–76
  market-implied forecast period in,
    73
  nonoperating assets and debt in,
    72
  reading, 71–73
  revising, 76
probabilities, determining, 106–107
project volatility, 120, 123–124
  benchmarks for, 124–125
property rights, 138

Rappaport, Alfred, 157, 159
raw materials, 60
real estate market, 20
real-options analysis, 117–134
  of Amazon.com, 128–132
  forms of options in, 118–119
  lookup table for, 122–123, 124
  market-imputed value and,
    126–127
  potential versus imputed,
    125–128
  reflexivity and, 132–134
  start-ups and, 117–118

strategic-investment analogy to,
    119–122
  valuing options in, 122–125
  variables in, 120–121
  when to use, 125–128
reconfiguration, 146
reflexivity, 132–134
reinventors, 118
research-and-development
    spillovers, 144–145
residual income, 192
residual value
  estimating, 26–27, 36–38
  perpetuity method for, 36–37
  perpetuity-with-inflation method
    for, 37–38
retail banking, 145–146, 147
retail book industry, 62
revenue recognition, 11–12
risk, rate of return and, 29–31, 121
risk-free interest rate, 79
risk-free rate of return, 121
rivalry among firms, 56, 94
rival versus nonrival goods, 137–138
Rogers, Will, 90

sales growth
  at Gateway, 96, 101–103
  as value driver, 22–23
sales triggers, estimating, 87
Santa Clara University, 112
Sara Lee Corporation, 146
scalability, 137
sell decisions. *See* buy, sell, hold
    decisions
service companies, 136
Shapiro, Carl, 63
share buybacks, 171–183
  circumstances surrounding, 177
  versus dividends, 181–182

share buybacks (*continued*)
  golden rule of, 173–175
  increasing financial leverage with,
    182–183
  management signals in, 172–173
  managing earning per share with,
    178–180
  motivations for, 175–183
  as negative signal, 173
  rate of return from, 174
  returning cash to shareholders
    with, 180–182
  to signal undervaluation, 175–177
shareholder value. *See also* mergers
    and acquisitions
  cash flow in, 21–22
  versus corporate value, 33–34
  expectations changes effects on,
    47–48
  of Gateway, 99
  investment efficiencies and,
    147–149
  sales trigger and, 87
  sample calculation of, 34–35
shareholder value at risk (SVAR),
    157–160
Shefrin, Hersh, 91, 112
Sirower, Mark L., 157, 159
Slywotzky, Adrian, 44, 58, 60
software, up-front versus
    incremental costs of, 63. *See
    also* knowledge businesses
Soros, George, 132
Southwest Airlines, 44
stability, industry, 52–53
Standard & Poor's, 71
start-ups
  ESOs and, 80–81, 84
  real-options valuation of,
    117–118
  reflexivity and, 132–134

steel industry, 142–143
stock issuance, 162–163
stock offers, 162, 163–164
stock options. *See* employee stock
    options
stock prices, xv–xvii
  buy decisions and, 110–111
  cash flow impact on, 19–21
  corporate value and, 33–34
  cost of capital and, 28–32
  ESOs and, 79–84
  estimating expectations from,
    69–84
  expectations basis of, 19–21
  expectations implied by, 2
  forecast period and, 33
  free cash flow and, 22–28
  how the market creates, 19–38
  investing styles and, 6–7
  in management decisions, 3
  reaction to mergers/acquisitions
    of, 164–168
  reflexivity and, 132–134
  shareholder value and, 21–22,
    33–35
  target, 100
  volatility of, 123–124
substitution threat, 55, 93
sunk costs, 111–112
supplier power, 56, 93
synergies, 155–156
  evaluating current risk of,
    166–167
  measuring risk of, 157–162

target prices, 100
taxes
  book, 23–24
  cash, 23–24
  ESOs and, 83

sell decisions and, 113, 114–115
share buybacks and, 181, 182
technology
  disruptive, 61–63, 95
  distribution changes from, 59
  sustaining, 61
  value chain analysis and, 58–60
Thaler, Richard, 112
The Theory of Investment Value
  (Williams), 8
threshold margin, 47–48
  shareholder value and, 47–48
Treynor, Jack, 6
turbo trigger, 85
  estimating, 89–90
  selecting, 87–89, 99–101
Tversky, Amos, 113

uncertainty, xii–xiii
  increased, 3
  real-options analysis and, 125–126
U.S. Office of Technology
  Assessment, 143
U. S. Securities and Exchange
  Commission, fair disclosure, 3
user base, establishing, 64–65

value
  book versus market, 28–29
  corporate, 21, 33–34
  earnings growth and, 15–16
  expected-value analysis and, 107
  of flexibility, 119
  indicators of and incentive
    compensation, 193–194

leading indicators of, 89–90
of project, 120, 123
variability of, 107–108
value chain analysis, 58–60, 94–95
value drivers, 22–23
  in expectations revisions, 40–41
  historical analysis of, 52, 53
  share buybacks and, 173
value factors, 40–46
  business categories and,
    140–149
  competitive strategy analysis
    and, 52–53
  cost efficiencies, 44–45
  economies of scale, 43–44
  investment efficiencies, 45–46
  operating leverage, 42–43
  price and mix, 42
  volume, 42
value growth duration, 73
Value Line Investment Survey, 71
value triggers, 40–41, 46, 48–49
Varian, Hal, 63
Verlinden, Matt, 59
vertical integration, 58
volatility, 120, 123–125
volume
  business categories and,
    141–142
  as value factor, 42

Wall Street Journal, 178–179
Wal-Mart, 46
Welch, Jack, xi
Williams, John Burr, 8
Wurster, Thomas, 60

about the authors

Alfred Rappaport is the Leonard Spacek Professor Emeritus at Northwestern University's J.L. Kellogg Graduate School of Management, where he was a member of the faculty for twenty-eight years. His research focuses on the application of shareholder value to corporate planning, performance evaluation, and mergers and acquisitions. He is also Shareholder Value Adviser to L.E.K. Consulting. His widely acclaimed, pioneering book, *Creating Shareholder Value: The New Standard for Business Performance*, was published in 1986. An updated edition, *Creating Shareholder Value: A Guide for Managers and Investors*, was published in 1998. Rappaport has been a guest columnist for the *Wall Street Journal*, the *New York Times*, and *Business Week* and has contributed more than seventy articles to leading business and academic publications. He originated the *Wall Street Journal Shareholder Scoreboard*, a ranking by total shareholder returns of the 1,000 most valuable U.S. corporations, published annually since 1996. He lives in La Jolla, California.

Michael J. Mauboussin is a Managing Director and Chief U.S. Investment Strategist at Credit Suisse First Boston Corporation in New York City. He is an acknowledged leader in the application of the shareholder value approach to security analysis and has lectured and published widely on the subject. Mauboussin is an Adjunct Professor of Finance at the Columbia University Graduate School of Business, is a former President of the Consumer Analyst Group of New York, and has been repeatedly named to *Institutional Investor's* All-America Research Team and the *Wall Street Journal* All-Star Survey in the food industry category. He is also on the board of trustees at the Santa Fe Institute, a leading center for multidisciplinary research in complex systems theory. He lives in Darien, Connecticut.

related materials
by these authors

"Stock or Cash? The Trade-Offs for Buyers and Sellers in Mergers and Acquisitions"
Alfred Rappaport and Mark L. Sirower
Harvard Business Review, November–December 1999
Reprint 99611

"New Thinking on How to Link Executive Pay with Performance"
Alfred Rappaport
Harvard Business Review, March–April 1999
Reprint 99210

"CFOs and Strategists: Forging a Common Framework"
Alfred Rappaport
Harvard Business Review, May–June 1992
Reprint 92309

"The Staying Power of the Public Corporation"
Alfred Rappaport
Harvard Business Review, January–February 1990
Reprint 90110

"Stock Market Signals to Managers"
Alfred Rappaport
Harvard Business Review, November–December 1987
Reprint 87611

"Selecting Strategies That Create Shareholder Value"
Alfred Rappaport
Harvard Business Review, May–June 1981
Reprint 81310

"Strategic Analysis for More Profitable Acquisitions"
Alfred Rappaport
Harvard Business Review, July–August 1979
Reprint 79409

"Executive Incentives vs. Corporate Growth"
Alfred Rappaport
Harvard Business Review, July–August 1978
Reprint 78406

For more information or to download these articles from the Internet, please visit our Web site: www.hbsp.harvard.edu